Monday Morning COOKING CLUB

the food, the stories, the sisterhood

Merelyn Frank Chalmers, Natanya Eskin, Lauren Fink,
Lisa Goldberg, Paula Horwitz and Jacqui Israel

Photography by Alan Benson

HarperCollins*Publishers*

ACKNOWLEDGEMENTS

*From inception through to birth, the creation of this book has taken us on the most incredible journey.
It is with thanks to the wonderful people mentioned here, and many others too numerous to mention,
that we can finally deliver our bundle of joy.*

*Our great appreciation to the extraordinary publishing, creative and design team who each helped us produce
this equally extraordinary book, and along the way became part of our family: publisher Caroline Lowry,
stylist Sarah O'Brien, eagle-eyed editor Kim Rowney and designer Jay Ryves.
And photographer Alan Benson, who always went above and beyond his camera lens.*

*For so generously providing us with much-needed professional assistance, a multitude of thanks to
Andrew Silberberg and Matthew Morris (Arnold Bloch Leibler, Solicitors), Lawrence Myers and Jackie Merrigan
(MBP Advisory, Chartered Accountants), Linda Tate (The Tate Gallery), Tony Ryba (White International)
and Ezra Sarajinsky (Ezra By Design).*

*For wisdom, guidance and support when we could use it most, huge thanks to Cherie Bevan (Crave Wares),
Philip Carr, Albert Dadon, Jackie Frank, Helen Greenwood, David Kugel (Network Printing Studios), Judy and
Steven Lowy, Sean Moran, Indira Naidoo, Maeve O'Meara, Damien Pignolet, Carli Ratcliff, Julie Rosenberg,
Ingrid Shakenovsky, Peter Silver, Boaz Stark, Simon Thomsen and Judy Wilkenfeld.*

*Monday Morning Cooking Club is a not-for-profit company and 100 per cent of our profits from sales of this book
will go to charity. Our major beneficiaries are WIZO (www.wizoaustralia.org) and OzHarvest (www.ozharvest.org).
With much admiration and thanks to Anat Shechter, Esther Wakerman, Kerry Rabie, Nilly Berger and all the wonderful
ladies at WIZO NSW, Gilla Liberman (President, WIZO Australia), and Ronni Kahn (Founding Director, OzHarvest).*

*Most of all we want to thank our 65 cooks, who so generously shared their precious recipes with us — because their
stories and food give our book its soul.*

*And last, but certainly not least, many hugs and kisses to our six supportive husbands and seventeen spectacular
children who were greatly neglected along the way, but spoilt with vast quantities of delicious food.*

Monday Morning Cooking Club

CONTENTS

Our story

4

Who we are

6

The cooks, the stories, the recipes

Our book is ordered alphabetically by cook or, in some cases, a family of cooks. Each cook shares a short story of themselves, and the introduction to each recipe gives an insight into the dish.

8

Glossary

264

Index

266

International conversions

270

Our story

We started our journey in Sydney, Australia. We wanted to find the food for our soul – those hidden treasures, those recipes not to be lost, those recipes that tell the tale of a community.

Nurturing, feeding and nourishing those whom we love.
Eating, sharing and breaking bread together.

The Jewish people have an unusually strong, somewhat obsessive connection with food. Every festival, celebration and time of sorrow is marked by the creation and consumption of special dishes and foods.

If someone is ill, chicken soup is promptly made and delivered.

If someone dies, eggs are boiled and bagels are bought. No flowers are sent – a cake is baked.

If a baby is born, entire meals are prepared for entire families.

It is always about the food.

Recipes have been handed down since the beginning of time.

Recipes are shared and copied, made and remade, eaten and enjoyed, cherished and loved.

Recipes help us remember our parents, our grandparents and our old aunties who are no longer with us. They are the thread that connects us to the past, ensuring continuity.

Our aim was simple: to gather the best recipes from some of the best cooks in our wide and diverse community.

To give us an insight into what food feeds our soul.

To create a book that would serve not only as a snapshot of our cooking at this time, but also as an historical record of where our recipes came from and what they mean to us.

To give us an opportunity to permanently record all those recipes that might otherwise be forgotten or, at worst, buried along with the older generation.

To produce a record for our children and their children.

So how did we start?

We emailed everyone we knew and then everyone they knew, asking for the best home cooks in town. Many were recommended to us; very few volunteered themselves. We asked everyone we came across, 'Who is the best cook you know?' We asked again and again. Slowly but surely over many months, a list began to take shape. We wrote to each of these cooks and asked for their very best. The brief was that we needed the recipes they were known for, those dishes that have nourished their family and friends for years.

Those recipes from great-grandmothers, grandmothers and mothers.

Those recipes that have something special.

The recipes trickled in, slowly at first, and then gained momentum. Before we knew it we had hundreds. Each recipe selected was (in our humble opinion) the best of its kind.

We wanted it to have either a story or a history, or just be unique in itself.

We had to be able to follow the recipe and re-create it in our 'test kitchen'.

And so, the Monday Morning Cooking Club was born.

Every Monday morning for three years we met in Lisa's kitchen and we cooked.

We chopped and stirred, minced and rolled.
We roasted and baked, fried and boiled.
We tasted and we ate.
And we ate and we argued.
And we ate and we laughed.
And we ate and we debated.
In?
Not in.
Out?
Yes.
No.
Maybe.
Back to the start, let's try it again.

Months passed and a 'Yes' list began to form.
   We were so excited by the recipes and the wonderful cooks we had found, and felt honoured they had shared their treasured recipes with us.

For three years, we tested (and tested and tested again), and then refined some of the most wonderful recipes from so many diverse cooks. We were committed to ensuring that these recipes would work in any kitchen, and that cooks at every level could master them.

We hope that this book will become a cherished part of everyone's recipe book collection across Australia and the world.

No matter where you come from, this book is for your soul.
   We hope it will inspire you to return to your kitchen, to engage with your grandparents and grandchildren over the dining table, or to find your own sisterhood through cooking.
   And, most of all, to enjoy all these treasures of a very special community.

Happy cooking, happy eating and happy sharing.

Monday Morning Cooking Club

WHO WE ARE

Lisa Goldberg

The leader and driving force of the team. Abandoned her background in law and brings her passion and obsession with food to the club. With compelling enthusiasm, she expects perfection from herself and the girls in the test kitchen. Her occasional bossiness is forgiven. Lisa is truly committed to finding that ultimate collection of recipes and producing a cookbook that the whole world can enjoy.

Merelyn Frank Chalmers

A serious and talented cook, always in search of that perfect recipe, particularly the classic ones to go with her own classic style. When it comes to cooking, Merelyn insists on precision; when it comes to writing, she stews about dotting the 'i's and crossing the 't's'. Often wears her public relations hat to the sisterhood's table, easing the project along the right path.

Natanya Eskin

Loves the process of unearthing recipes from the older generations, and is just as fascinated with the stories they tell as what they cook. A background in teaching leads Natanya to question everything, and she regularly plays devil's advocate to bring out the best in the group, often setting a debate raging. Shows an impassioned and unwavering faith that the girls have the collective ability to produce an outstanding book.

Lauren Fink

A tireless charity worker and fundraiser who stands up strong and proud of her Jewish heritage. For Lauren, being part of this project supports both these pursuits. She never lets the group forget their roots and what a difference they can make to those in need, which helps sharpen the club's focus along the way. Cooks for a crowd with great warmth and style; no-one ever leaves hungry.

Paula Horwitz

Previously relegated to salad duty by her family, her newfound love of cooking now sees her army of boys devour her food. Paula and her husband, as new immigrants from South Africa, created the Bayswiss empire from one deli and a furniture shop. She has a good 'business' head on her shoulders and enviable computer skills, balancing well with her wry sense of humour.

Jacqui Israel

Ensures the smooth running of the group, always in a lighthearted way. She is detailed and methodical, recording everything in her little black book. Jacqui wasn't originally keen on cooking but, being a photography enthusiast, she has been busy documenting the club's journey – just for the record. Has finally accepted that she is part of the sisterhood for life. And now, she loves to cook!

Freda Abram

Probably as a result of growing up through the war, my parents were totally obsessed with food — preparing it, serving it and, of course, eating it. As a child, I remember their constant catchcry was, 'Come and eat!' My mother grew up in Poland and, like most women of her time, was expected to stay at home, help with the general running of the household, and cook.

My mother met my father after the war, when he was a patient in a hospital in Munich, where she worked as a nurse. They married and made plans to move to America, but sadly my father passed away. My mother, on her own with my brother and me, decided instead to immigrate to Australia with her brother. In Melbourne, she found love again and remarried.

I came to Sydney in 1973 to visit my brother, and then and there decided to stay. Our mother missed us terribly, so would visit three times a year, always bringing her trusty worn-out bag, bulging with our favourite dishes: gefilte fish, pelushki and almond torte. These are the three dishes that remind me so much of her.

I've always been interested in cooking and as I get older and have more time on my hands, my enjoyment grows. My mother didn't actively teach me to cook; I learnt by simply standing beside her and watching. My husband and I have two children, who both love to cook. Sasha says that she missed the opportunity to learn from her grandmother, who passed away in 1998, and now she has to learn from other people's grandmothers instead.

Pelushki is the one dish that most reminds me of my mum, Hala. Pelushki are really authentic Polish food, a type of dumpling made with potatoes and onions. She made them for almost any occasion, and how we devoured those little fluffy pillows smothered in golden fried onions, always served with a glass of buttermilk. I also love making them and now my daughter makes them, too. And she will, in time, teach her kids to make them, and Hala's memory will live on in generations to come.

PELUSHKI

40 G BUTTER

60 ML (¼ CUP) VEGETABLE OIL

4 BROWN ONIONS, CHOPPED

3 PONTIAC OR BRUSHED POTATOES
   (700 G IN TOTAL), PEELED AND
   QUARTERED

150 G (1 CUP) PLAIN FLOUR

½ TEASPOON SALT

1 EGG

EXTRA FLOUR, FOR KNEADING
   AND ROLLING

In a large frying pan, heat the butter and oil on a medium–high heat. Add the onions and fry for 10 minutes, or until dark golden. Set aside in the pan.

Boil the potatoes in plenty of water for 30 minutes until soft, then drain well. Grate the warm potatoes into a large bowl. Add the flour and salt, mix through lightly and make a well in the centre. Crack the egg into the well, beat it lightly with a fork, then use your hands to mix together for a minute or so until the dough just comes together. If it is too dry, add another egg. Tip the potato mixture onto a very well floured (at least ¼ cup) surface and knead very lightly for about 1 minute, just until you have a workable dough. Be careful not to overwork the dough.

Take a handful of the dough and shape it into a rectangle, about 1.5 cm thick. With a well-floured knife, cut the rectangle into 1.5 cm wide strips, and then cut the strips into 1 cm pieces to make small gnocchi-like dumplings. Alternatively, you can roll the dough into a small sausage, about 1 cm in diameter, and then cut it into small pieces. Keep the dumplings on a floured board until ready to cook.

Bring a large saucepan or stockpot of salted water to the boil and put the dumplings in the water. A couple of minutes after they float to the surface, they are ready. Taste one to test it is cooked through. Remove with a slotted spoon.

While the dumplings are cooking, reheat the onions in the frying pan. Put the cooked dumplings into the pan with the hot onions and toss gently to combine. Remove from the pan and serve with a glass of cold buttermilk. The dumplings are also great served as gnocchi with the sauce of your choice.

Serves 6

Agi Adler

Before I married I had never cooked. When I first arrived in Sydney I worked at a tailors in the Strand Arcade, and it was there I met Bob, a German refugee. We fell in love and married. At the beginning of our marriage my poor husband suffered through quite a lot of my cooking trials and errors as I found my feet in the kitchen. But I kept on and soon discovered I had quite a passion for cooking, and especially enjoyed re-creating the food from my childhood in Hungary, the wonderful schnitzel and csipetke dumplings that my grandmother and mother used to make.

Cooking takes me back to my home, it reminds me of my history, culture and, importantly, the people I loved. I lost both my parents in the war, so I lived with my grandmother for a time in our family flat in Budapest. I was eighteen when I was offered an opportunity to travel overseas to start a new life, and I took the chance. After waiting for my papers in Paris for six months, I left for Australia and arrived in Sydney in April 1949.

Now there is nothing I love more than cooking for my family, and sharing my recipes with my two daughters. It gives me great pleasure to know that they will continue to pass these skills and my history on to their families.

This is a very traditional recipe I picked up from looking in books and talking to other Hungarians, as I wanted to re-create the tastes of my youth. Csipetke (pronounced chi-pet-kee) means 'little pinches' in Hungarian. Essentially they are a cross between a little dumpling and a noodle. If you do not keep kosher, stir in 1 tablespoon of sour cream just before serving.

BEAN SOUP WITH CSIPETKE

500 G (2½ CUPS) DRIED
   CANNELLINI BEANS, SOAKED
   OVERNIGHT IN WATER
3 LARGE CARROTS, PEELED AND
   FINELY DICED
1 TABLESPOON SALT
500 G SMOKED RIBS OR SMOKED
   SAUSAGE, CUT INTO 5 MM SLICES
   (OR SMOKED BRISKET, ROUGHLY
   DICED)
60 ML (¼ CUP) VEGETABLE OIL
2 TABLESPOONS PLAIN FLOUR
1 TABLESPOON PAPRIKA

CSIPETKE
175 G PLAIN FLOUR
PINCH OF SALT
1 EGG
1–1½ TABLESPOONS WATER

Start this recipe the day before, soaking the beans. The next day, drain the beans and place in a large stockpot with the carrots. Cover with enough water so there is 5 cm on top. Bring to the boil, then reduce the heat and simmer for 30 minutes, or until the beans are semi-soft. Add the salt and meat and continue to cook for about 30 minutes, or until both the beans and meat are soft. If the soup is too thick to stir easily, add more water.

While the soup is cooking, make the csipetke dough. Sift the flour and salt into a bowl and make a small well. Add the egg and 1 tablespoon of the water and knead until you have a stiff dough. If the dough is too dry, add a little more water. Flatten the dough between your palms, then pinch off small bean-sized pieces of dough. Lay them on a floured board until you are ready to cook them.

In a frying pan, mix the oil and flour together and cook on a medium heat until a golden brown roux (paste) is formed. Take the pan off the heat and stir in the paprika, then add the roux to the soup, stirring well. The soup will thicken slightly.

Bring the soup up to simmering point, drop the dough pieces into the soup and cook for a further 15–20 minutes, or until the csipetke are cooked through.

Serves 8–10

I came across this recipe many years ago. It isn't Hungarian, but it has become a family favourite, particularly with my son-in-law Rob, who loves it because it reminds him of his Polish grandmother's recipe for chocolate cake. We tried her old handwritten recipe many times, but could never get it to work because the ingredients were 'a little of this' and 'a little of that', so it was exciting for him to stumble across a cake that captured the flavours of the 'old country'. In our family when it's your birthday you get to choose your cake, and Rob always picks this one. This recipe can be made two days ahead.

CHERRY, ALMOND AND CHOCOLATE CAKE

720 G JAR SOUR CHERRIES
200 G UNSALTED BUTTER,
   AT ROOM TEMPERATURE
230 G (1 CUP) CASTER SUGAR
4 EGGS
200 G (2 CUPS) GROUND ALMONDS
   (ALMOND MEAL)
100 G DARK CHOCOLATE, GRATED
2 TABLESPOONS RUM (OR JUICE
   FROM THE CHERRIES)
75 G (½ CUP) SELF-RAISING
   FLOUR, SIFTED
1 TEASPOON GROUND CINNAMON
ICING SUGAR, FOR DUSTING

Preheat the oven to 180°C. Grease a 26 cm round cake tin and line the base with baking paper.

Drain the cherries, reserving the juice if necessary. Place the cherries on paper towel and pat dry.

Beat the butter and sugar together until light and fluffy. Add the eggs one at a time, beating after each addition until just combined. Stir in the ground almonds, chocolate, rum (or cherry juice), flour and cinnamon, then add the cherries. Pour the mixture into the prepared tin and bake for 55 minutes, or until a skewer inserted into the cake comes out clean. If the cake is overbrowning, cover the tin loosely with foil.

Leave the cake to cool in the tin for 5 minutes before turning out onto a wire rack. Serve the cake warm or cooled, dusted with sifted icing sugar.

Serves 10–12

Lyndi Adler

I grew up in Melbourne in a close-knit family, who loved nothing better than sitting down to eat together every night. There were usually four courses: an appetiser, soup, main course and, naturally, dessert. The food was typically Eastern European, prepared by my Czech-born mother and grandmother, who had survived the horrors of the Holocaust, arriving in Melbourne with my dad in 1949.

When it came to school lunches, my tub of leftover layered potatoes or rye bread sandwiches filled with Liptauer cheese dip would often remain untouched in the bottom of my bag, and instead I lusted after my best friend's white bread Vegemite sandwiches. But at home I loved that there was always a pot of soup on the stove, a fridge full of deli treats and delectable leftovers, and a pantry that boasted at least two home-baked cakes on any day of the week. Now, living in Sydney with my own family, my kitchen still reflects the one in which I grew up.

What to do with all that Friday night leftover chicken soup? Well, since Dad was a soup lover and we had soup six times a week, what better way to use it than to make another soup? We always had vegetables in the fridge and barley in the pantry, so all Mum needed to do was make a quick visit to the kosher butcher for the shanks. As children, this was one of our favourites — thick, warm and so nourishing.

VEAL SHANK AND BARLEY SOUP

2 TABLESPOONS OLIVE OIL

2 WHOLE VEAL SHANKS, EACH CUT INTO 3 PIECES

1 ONION, FINELY CHOPPED

3 STALKS CELERY, FINELY CHOPPED

4 CARROTS, PEELED AND FINELY CHOPPED

2 POTATOES (OPTIONAL), PEELED AND CUBED

2 LITRES (8 CUPS) GOOD-QUALITY CHICKEN STOCK

250 G FINE PEARL BARLEY

Heat 1 tablespoon of the olive oil in a large stockpot and sear the shank pieces on a high heat until browned all over. Remove from the pot and set aside.

Add the remaining oil to the pot and fry the onion and celery for 10 minutes until translucent and soft. Add the carrots (and potatoes if using). Season with salt and pepper and stir well.

Return the shanks to the pot and add enough stock to cover, then pour in the barley. Bring to the boil, stirring occasionally. Reduce the heat to a simmer, cover with a lid and cook for a further 2 hours, or until the shank meat falls off the bone. If the soup looks too thick, add additional stock or water.

When the shanks are cooked, remove them from the soup. When they are cool enough to handle, pull the meat from the bones, discarding the bones. Shred the meat and return it to the soup. Season to taste before serving.

Serves 10–12

When I was a child I was allowed the occasional small treat from a cake shop, but a bought cake would never do in our home: that was tantamount to insult, as both my mother and grandmother were excellent bakers. This simple but lovely cake is our family's staple cake; it is always in the house at any given time. There are many versions of this type of cake, but this one is not only foolproof it's also very delicious.

CHOCOLATE CHIFFON CAKE

260 g (1¾ cups) SELF-RAISING
    FLOUR
135 g (1 cup) DRINKING
    CHOCOLATE
6 EGGS, SEPARATED
345 g (1½ cups) CASTER SUGAR
250 ML (1 cup) VEGETABLE OIL
250 ML (1 cup) HOT TAP WATER

Preheat the oven to 180°C. You will need an angel cake (chiffon) tin (see note, page 35). Do not grease it.

Sift together the flour and drinking chocolate and set aside. Whisk the egg whites until soft peaks form, then slowly add half of the sugar. Continue whisking until stiff peaks form, then set aside.

Beat the egg yolks with the remaining sugar until pale and very fluffy. Slowly add the oil and continue to beat. Fold in the flour mixture, alternating with the hot water, and beat together for a few minutes. Gently fold the egg whites into the chocolate mixture until just combined. Pour into the cake tin and bake for 1 hour.

After removing the cake from the oven, immediately invert it to cool by balancing the middle funnel onto a bottle neck. It is important for the cake to be inverted and suspended upside down until it is cool to stop it from collapsing. When cool, run a knife around the outside of the cake and around the funnel. Lift the base out of the tin, then use the knife to ease the cake off the base.

Serves 12

My mother always wrote this as 'plumb' cake, and it wasn't until I was well into my teenage years that I realised she had spelled it incorrectly. It is now always fondly remembered as Mum's 'plumb' cake. This is an old Eastern European recipe that has been in my family for many years. This cake always causes much excitement in our household, as it heralds the start of summer and the much-awaited arrival of stone fruit.

'PLUMB' CAKE

DOUGH
225 G (1½ CUPS) PLAIN FLOUR
225 G (1½ CUPS) SELF-RAISING
    FLOUR
250 G UNSALTED BUTTER, CHOPPED
230 G (1 CUP) CASTER SUGAR
3 EGG YOLKS
150 G SOUR CREAM

CRUMBLE
300 G (2 CUPS) PLAIN FLOUR
345 G (1½ CUPS) CASTER SUGAR
190 G UNSALTED BUTTER, CHOPPED
12–16 BLOOD PLUMS (OR ENOUGH
    TO ALMOST FILL THE TIN),
    WASHED, HALVED AND STONES
    REMOVED
CINNAMON SUGAR, FOR
    SPRINKLING

Start this recipe the day before serving. To make the dough, put the flours and butter in a bowl and use your fingertips to mix them together, until the butter is evenly dispersed and the mixture forms crumbs. Add the sugar, egg yolks and sour cream and mix together using your hands or a wooden spoon. When a soft, sticky ball of dough is formed, wrap in plastic and refrigerate overnight.

To make the crumble, use your fingertips or a food processor to combine the flour, sugar and butter until crumbs form. Refrigerate until needed. Remove the dough from the fridge 30 minutes before using.

Preheat the oven to 180°C. Grease a 28–30 cm springform cake tin. On a well-floured surface, roll out the dough thickly, to fit the base and halfway up the side of the tin. Line the base and side of the tin with the dough, then place the plums on top, arranging them very close together. With your hands, squeeze the crumble mixture together, then break it up over the top of the plums. Sprinkle with the cinnamon sugar and bake for 1½ hours, or until the cake is golden on top and cooked through. Serve warm or at room temperature with cream or ice cream.

Serves 12

My parents were part of a tight circle of newly immigrated Czechs, and this was one of the recipes that 'went around' to everyone's house. This is my family's version. I have such warm memories of standing next to my mother and 'aunty' Lily in the kitchen during the Yom Kippur breaking-of-the-fast meal. At least twenty family and friends sat around our dining-room table and feasted, while they methodically cooked a pancake, sprinkled the nuts, cooked another layer and so on, until finally, they proudly carried the puffed and tantalising dessert to the table.

SOUFFLÉ PANCAKES

130 g (1 cup) COARSELY GROUND
   WALNUTS
160 g (1 cup) ICING SUGAR, MIXED
   WITH 25 g (1 SACHET) VANILLA
   SUGAR (SEE NOTE, PAGE 150)
6 EGGS, SEPARATED
3 TABLESPOONS CASTER SUGAR
40 g UNSALTED BUTTER, MELTED
3 TABLESPOONS PLAIN FLOUR,
   SIFTED
300 ML MILK

Preheat the oven to 180°C. Grease a baking dish large enough to fit a stack of 10–12 pancakes.

Mix together the ground walnuts and icing sugar mixture and set aside. Whisk the egg whites with 1 tablespoon of the sugar until soft peaks form. In a separate bowl, beat the egg yolks with the remaining sugar, then stir in the melted butter, flour and milk. Fold this mixture into the egg whites.

Generously grease a medium crepe pan and then place on a medium heat. Pour in about one ladleful of pancake mixture and swirl it around to cover the base of the pan. Fry the pancake on one side only; when it is just set on top, carefully slide it into the prepared baking dish, with the uncooked side facing up. Sprinkle with a few teaspoons of the walnut and icing sugar mixture. Continue to cook and layer the pancakes, sprinkling the mixture between each pancake, finishing with the mixture on the top. Place the dish in the oven and bake for 20 minutes. Cut into wedges to serve.

Serves 8–10

Variation: Instead of using the walnut and icing sugar mixture between the pancakes, substitute drinking chocolate or grated good-quality dark chocolate.

Manya Boorda

Known fondly to her family and friends as Booby, Manya was born in a little shtetl in the Ukraine in 1910. When she was eight, Manya and her mother fled from the pogroms, spending a year on the road until they reached Harbin in China. She lived there with her mother and aunties, learning her cooking skills from them.

At the age of sixteen, Manya married and had a son, John. John immigrated to Australia in 1948 and his parents followed soon after. He could not remember his mother, grandmother or even great-grandmother ever needing to consult a cookbook; everything was handed down from one generation to the next. One person would cook the food and then someone else did the tasting, suggesting perhaps 'a bissel more of this and a bissel more of that'. It was always done from memory and then by taste.

Manya loved entertaining and regularly had a table bursting with food. To start, there was vodka and then at least a dozen zacuskas (appetisers). This was followed by a soup course and then, when everyone had eaten more than enough, the main course would arrive. After that there were cakes, pancakes and other sweets, followed with a cup of chai or tea. Of course nothing was too much trouble; it was always her pleasure. Manya, who passed away in 2005, loved it that her son John (who passed away in 2010), several grandchildren and great grandchildren all lived in Sydney together. They all smile when they think of her favourite expression: 'Please have a little more.'

Borscht is as much a part of the Russian culture as matzo ball soup is for the Jewish people. During the revolution and the pogroms, food was scarce. Hot borscht with potatoes and black bread (white bread was a luxury) was a great meal, particularly in winter. In warmer weather, cold borscht was the go. All Russian families knew how to make borscht and most tasted the same, although Booby's was the best of course! In those days chicken soup was a luxury, so this was a great alternative. Unlike chicken soup, it does not claim to cure any ailments, but it sure doesn't hurt. As the saying went: 'Just have more borscht.'

BOOBY'S HOT BORSCHT

1 LITRE (4 CUPS) CHICKEN STOCK
2 LITRES (8 CUPS) WATER
1.5 KG BEEF SPARE RIB OR TOP RIB
(OR OTHER MEAT ON THE BONE
SUITABLE FOR SOUPS)
4 FRESH BEETROOT, PEELED AND
ROUGHLY CHOPPED
850 G TIN WHOLE BEETROOT,
GRATED
2 LARGE CARROTS, PEELED AND
SLICED
4 POTATOES, PEELED AND CUT
INTO LARGE CUBES
400 G TIN DICED TOMATOES
410 G TIN TOMATO PURÉE
2 LEMONS, JUICED
1 TABLESPOON SUGAR
½ CABBAGE, SHREDDED

Put the stock and water into a large stockpot. Add the meat and bring to the boil, skimming the surface to remove the scum. Add the fresh and tinned beetroot, carrots, potatoes, tomatoes and tomato purée and boil for 1 hour, or until the meat is just about falling off the bone. Add the lemon juice and season with salt, pepper and sugar to balance the flavours. Add the cabbage and simmer for at least another 15 minutes, or until the cabbage is very soft.

Remove the meat from the saucepan. When cool enough to handle, pull the meat from the bones. Shred the meat with a fork and return it to the pan. Taste again and adjust the seasoning and lemon juice if necessary. Let the borscht cool overnight. The next day, skim off any fat and reheat to serve.

Serves 12

Booby's traditional cold borscht

4 FRESH BEETROOT
2 LITRES (8 CUPS) WATER
2 TABLESPOONS SUGAR, PLUS
    EXTRA TO TASTE
2 TABLESPOONS FRESHLY
    SQUEEZED LEMON JUICE, PLUS
    EXTRA TO TASTE
1 TEASPOON SALT, PLUS EXTRA
    TO TASTE
850 G TIN WHOLE BEETROOT,
    GRATED
3 EGGS

CONDIMENTS
2 CUCUMBERS, DICED
2 HARD-BOILED EGGS, CHOPPED
SOUR CREAM
1 SMALL BUNCH SPRING ONIONS,
    FINELY CHOPPED

Peel the fresh beetroot and cut into quarters. Place it in a saucepan and cover with 1.5 litres (6 cups) of the water. Bring to the boil and cook for about 45 minutes, or until soft. Remove the beetroot from the water, reserving the water in the saucepan.

Grate the cooked beetroot into a large bowl and add the sugar, lemon juice and salt. Taste for balance, adding a little more of each if necessary. Return this mixture to the saucepan with the reserved cooking water in it. Add the remaining 500 ml (2 cups) of water to the pan along with the grated tinned beetroot and bring to the boil.

Beat the eggs in a large mixing bowl. Slowly spoon about a third of the hot soup into the eggs, one spoonful at a time. Keep beating the eggs, making sure they do not curdle. Add the remainder of the soup to the bowl and season with salt, pepper, sugar and lemon juice, to taste. If you prefer a smoother borscht, transfer the soup to a food processor and purée. Allow to cool and then refrigerate. Serve cold, with the condiments on the side.

Serves 8

Philip Carr

My food philosophy is to always select the best possible and seasonal ingredients, and to prepare and serve them with the best accompaniments — top-quality olive oils, vinegars, breads, chocolate, and so on. I take a somewhat holistic approach to food and cooking. It is of course about the food, but also the aesthetics of the particular dish, the platter it sits on, the tablecloth and the surrounding environment.

I love my work as an event organiser. I can trace my interest back to the days of growing up in Johannesburg. Sunday was my favourite day — our family day by the pool. I was in awe of my mother getting up early and spending the entire morning organising, preparing and cooking; she was truly a wonderful entertainer who did so with great ease and joy. One weekend I offered to help her with a friend's major event. I started moving tables and carrying everything that was needed, then soon I was telling her where to put the tables, and making suggestions about the layout and style. That's where it all began and before I knew it I was catering and putting together all manner of parties, events and celebrations. When Sydney became my home in the 1990s, I kept doing what I loved best. I have made cooking for friends my hobby, and helping clients create magnificent events my vocation.

I was given this recipe many years ago, and have made it so many times that it has become my signature dish and an annual ritual when artichoke season comes around. This is how I love to entertain at home — sitting around the table with a group of friends, a crusty loaf of bread and the large pot of artichokes in the middle, with everyone chatting, sharing and eating together. This dish is best made the day before and gently reheated, or served at room temperature.

ARTICHOKE STEW

2 LEMONS

8 LARGE ARTICHOKES

80 ML (⅓ CUP) OLIVE OIL

80 G (1 SMALL JAR) ANCHOVIES

16 FRENCH ESCHALOTS,
   BLANCHED, PEELED AND LEFT
   WHOLE

4 CLOVES GARLIC, CRUSHED

16 SMALL POTATOES, PEELED AND
   HALVED

3 LEMONS, EXTRA, CUT INTO
   5 MM SLICES OR HALVED, SEEDS
   REMOVED

1 LITRE (4 CUPS) CHICKEN STOCK

1 KG FRESH BROAD BEANS,
   PODDED, THEN COOKED
   (SEE NOTE)

1 BUNCH DILL, CHOPPED, TO
   SERVE (OPTIONAL)

Fill a large bowl with water. Cut the lemons in half and squeeze the juice into the water, then put the lemons into the bowl as well. You need to have this bowl of acidulated water ready before you prepare the artichokes, as they discolour very quickly.

Remove the tough outer leaves of the artichoke. Peel the rough outside of the stalk with a paring knife, and trim to about 5 cm in length. Cut about 3 cm off the top of the artichoke by slicing across the leaves with a sharp knife. Slice the artichoke vertically in half, then use a teaspoon to remove the centre choke. Place the artichoke in the acidulated water, and repeat. Drain and dry the artichokes well on paper towel before using.

The next stage has to be done in three or four batches, depending on the size of your pan. Heat some of the olive oil in a large frying pan and sauté some of the anchovies and eschalots on a medium–high heat for about 15 minutes, or until the anchovies have melted and the eschalots are golden. Add some of the garlic, potatoes, lemon slices and artichokes and sauté on a high heat for about 10 minutes until brown. Remove from the pan and set aside. Repeat until all are browned.

Place a very large stockpot or flameproof casserole dish on the stovetop. Put all the browned ingredients into the pot. Pour in the stock and simmer, uncovered, for 30 minutes, or until the artichokes and potatoes are tender. Add the broad beans and toss through, taking care not to break the artichoke stems. Allow to cool. Season well to taste, and sprinkle with dill to serve if you wish. Serve with crusty bread.

Serves 8

Note: To cook the broad beans, boil for 3 minutes, then drain. When cool enough to handle, squeeze the beans out of the skins (to give about 150 g double-shelled broad beans).

This is the most decadent and rich dessert, perfect to follow a light main course. Several years ago for my fortieth birthday in London, I wanted a quick but perfect dessert. Thinking I might make a bread and butter pudding, I ran out to the shops, but all I could find were croissants and Valrhona chocolate — and that's how it started. I made the pudding and everyone raved. It is so easy to make and serve; put the dish in the middle of the table for everyone to tear off chunks of chocolate-soaked croissant, bit by bit. When my friends travel from London, the first thing they ask is: 'When are we coming around for your pudding?'

CHOCOLATE 'BREAD AND BUTTER' PUDDING

150 G BEST-QUALITY DARK
   CHOCOLATE, CHOPPED
425 ML PURE CREAM (35% FAT)
2 TABLESPOONS DARK RUM
115 G (½ CUP) CASTER SUGAR
75 G UNSALTED BUTTER, CHOPPED
PINCH OF GROUND CINNAMON
3 EGGS
9 CROISSANTS, EACH CUT INTO
   4 PIECES
COCOA POWDER OR ICING SUGAR,
   FOR DUSTING

Start this recipe the day before. Grease an ovenproof dish, approximately 28 x 24 x 7 cm, to fit the croissants snugly.

Place the chocolate, cream, rum, sugar, butter and cinnamon in a double boiler or in a heatproof bowl over a saucepan of simmering water. Heat gently until the chocolate is melted and all the ingredients are dissolved. Remove from the heat. Whisk the eggs in a bowl and then beat into the chocolate mixture.

Spoon a little of the chocolate mixture into the baking dish and add the croissants, in overlapping layers, starting with the middle slices at the bottom of the dish, cut side up, and finishing with the croissant ends sticking up vertically (for a better visual effect). Pour the remaining mixture evenly over the croissants. Cover with plastic wrap and place in the fridge for 24 hours.

When you are ready to serve, preheat the oven to 180°C. Cover the dish with foil and bake for 25 minutes, then remove the foil and cook for a further 10 minutes. Remove from the oven and let the pudding rest for 10 minutes before serving. Dust with cocoa or icing sugar and serve with vanilla bean ice cream or cream.

Serves 12–16

Merelyn Chalmers

My kitchen is the link between the old world and the new. I may have been born in Western Australia, but the salt and pepper of my home life was Judaism and Yiddishkeit. My parents immigrated to Australia individually, from Poland and Hungary, and met in Perth. They both came from observant families, but from completely different food cultures, so there was constant haranguing over which country made the best gefilte fish and matzo balls.

My elder brother and I were involved in the kitchen from a young age. There was an order to the apprenticeship. At first I was only allowed to flour the schnitzel, while Mark egged and breadcrumbed, and Mum fried. As we got older, Mark was allowed to fry and I took over the egg and breadcrumbs. Then, finally, it was my turn to take the helm. Being in charge of frying had major privileges. I would sneak a small piece of schnitzel straight from the pan and eat it, searing hot. I burnt my tongue every time but it was always worth it — the crunch of the breadcrumbs, the tender hot meat and the steam warming my face is still scorched in my memory.

As I left the food culture of my youth and began to explore French, Italian and Moroccan cooking, my mother came along for the ride, adding more cuisines to her cooking repertoire. Always busy cooking, she poured her love into food and entertaining over Shabbat dinner. Now she has passed away, but I still find myself talking to her in the kitchen, just like we used to.

My own cooking can be light and contemporary or rustic and rough. I love baking cakes, and fill my kids' lunchboxes with homemade almost-healthy treats. Every now and then I crave Mum's famous Hungarian tortes and force-feed them to all those around me, just like she did.

My mother always made this for me when I was a child and not feeling well. It's a bit like Hungarian risotto and is so warming in the belly. It's certainly not glamorous, but it is delicious.

MUM'S RICE PAPRIKASH

80 ML (⅓ CUP) OLIVE OIL

1 KG VEAL SHIN (OFF THE BONE),
    CUT INTO LARGE DICE

3 LARGE ONIONS (500 G),
    VERY FINELY CHOPPED

60 ML (¼ CUP) WHITE WINE

500 ML (2 CUPS) BOILING WATER

2 CLOVES GARLIC, CRUSHED

1 RED CAPSICUM, SLICED

1 HEAPED TABLESPOON MILD
    PAPRIKA

¼ TEASPOON CAYENNE PEPPER,
    OR TO TASTE

220 G (1 CUP) LONG-GRAIN RICE

2 CARROTS, PEELED AND CUT INTO
    CHUNKS

1 SMALL TOMATO, CHOPPED

Heat the olive oil in a frying pan on a medium-high heat and fry the veal until very brown. Remove from the pan and set aside. Add the onions to the pan and fry until very brown, adding more oil if necessary.

Return the veal to the pan and add the wine and boiling water. Add the garlic, capsicum, paprika and cayenne pepper. Bring to the boil, then reduce the heat and simmer for 30 minutes.

Add the rice, carrots and tomato, stir to combine, then continue to simmer for a further 30 minutes, or until the veal is tender and the rice is cooked. Stir regularly and add more boiling water as required. Season to taste with salt and freshly ground black pepper.

Serves 6

This was my favourite cake when I was young, and now it's my children's favourite, too. I remember eating it in the kitchen after school and calling it 'yellow cake' because of its deep buttery colour. This has been my mother's secret recipe for close to fifty years. Many, many people have asked for the recipe, but until the Monday Morning Cooking Club, no-one was allowed a copy of it! Chiffon cake must be inverted while cooling to stop it from collapsing, so before you start check you have a bottle that fits in the funnel of the angel cake tin and that it will balance.

CUSTARD CHIFFON CAKE

175 G (1⅙ CUPS) SELF-RAISING
   FLOUR
1 TEASPOON CREAM OF TARTAR
35 G (¼ CUP) CUSTARD POWDER
6 LARGE EGGS, SEPARATED
345 G (1½ CUPS) CASTER SUGAR
½ TEASPOON VANILLA EXTRACT
80 ML (⅓ CUP) EXTRA LIGHT OLIVE
   OIL OR VEGETABLE OIL
170 ML (⅔ CUP) WARM WATER

Preheat the oven to 180°C. You will need an angel cake (chiffon) tin (see note). Do not grease it.

Sift the flour, cream of tartar and custard powder together three times to ensure they are fully combined.

In an electric mixer, beat the egg yolks with 230 g (1 cup) of the sugar until pale and creamy, then add the vanilla. Pour the oil and warm water into a jug. While the yolks are still beating on low speed, add the flour mixture and the oil and water at the same time, beating until just incorporated.

In a separate bowl, whisk the egg whites until soft peaks form, then add the remaining sugar and continue to whisk until the egg whites are stiff but not dry. Very carefully fold the batter into the egg whites with a metal spoon until just incorporated. Pour the mixture into the cake tin. Bake for 1 hour, or until a skewer comes out clean when inserted into the cake.

After removing the cake from the oven, immediately invert it to cool by balancing the middle funnel onto a bottle neck. (The cake will be dangling upside down.) It is important for the cake to be inverted and suspended upside down until it is cool to stop it from collapsing. When cool, run a knife around the outside of the cake and the funnel. Lift the base out of the tin, then use the knife to ease the cake off the base.

Serves 12

Note: For the best results, you need to use a high-sided cake tin (25 cm x 10 cm deep) with an inner funnel and removable base; do not use a non-stick tin. It is important to use an ungreased cake tin, which will allow the batter to cling to the side of the tin as it rises.

I grew up in Perth with no blood relatives except my direct nuclear family. But my 'aunty' Ruth and 'uncle' Graham and their kids are my family — without the baggage! Aunty Ruth was the first 'modern' cook I knew. Her Shabbat table featured foods of the 1970s, which were then updated to the '80s and '90s as time went on. Her lemon cream is one of my favourites. She serves it from a large bowl, accompanied with lightly sugared strawberries. I like to set it in individual glasses and then place mixed berries on top.

AUNTY RUTH'S LEMON CREAM

60 ML (¼ CUP) BOILING WATER
2 TEASPOONS POWDERED GELATINE
4 EGGS
230 G (1 CUP) CASTER SUGAR
140 ML FRESHLY SQUEEZED LEMON
   JUICE
300 ML PURE CREAM (35% FAT)
MIXED BERRIES, TO SERVE

Put the boiling water in a heatproof bowl and sprinkle over the gelatine, stirring until the gelatine is dissolved.

Beat the eggs and sugar together until very pale, light and fluffy. Add the lemon juice and dissolved gelatine and continue to beat until well combined. Pour the mixture into a bowl and place in the fridge for 2–3 hours until almost set.

Add the cream to the lemon mixture and beat again until well incorporated and as fluffy as possible. It will not be thick like whipped cream, but will hold air. Pour the lemon cream into a large serving bowl or individual ramekins. Return to the fridge for about 3 hours until set, or leave overnight. Serve with the mixed berries.

Serves 8–10

Barbara Cohen

I think it is wonderful to continue the tradition of passing down marvellous recipes, both traditional and contemporary, from generation to generation. I grew up in Cape Town, and as a child had little interest in what went on in my mum's kitchen. It wasn't until after I married that I developed a love of cooking and baking, and my mother was only too happy to guide me along the way. My first exposure to traditional Eastern European cooking came from my mother-in-law who, in the style of most cooks of her day, never wrote down her recipes. Sometimes, frustratingly, it was a bit of guesswork when it came to 'a pinch of this' and 'a handful of that'.

We immigrated to Sydney in 1990, and since then I have collected recipes from here, there and everywhere, building up a large repertoire of favourites. There's always something new to try out, and I love the creativity it gives me.

This delicious Mediterranean-style dish has been enjoyed on many a cold night by my family and friends. Add or substitute other seafood if you like.

MEDITERRANEAN FISH STEW WITH COUSCOUS

60 ML (¼ CUP) OLIVE OIL
1 ONION, FINELY CHOPPED
3 CLOVES GARLIC, FINELY CHOPPED
1 TEASPOON EACH FENNEL,
    CUMIN AND CORIANDER SEEDS,
    TOASTED AND GROUND
400 G TIN DICED ITALIAN TOMATOES
2 TABLESPOONS TOMATO PASTE
125 ML (½ CUP) FISH OR
    VEGETABLE STOCK
1 TEASPOON SUGAR
1 KG FIRM WHITE FISH, SKIN
    REMOVED AND SLICED INTO
    SMALL FILLETS

COUSCOUS
230 G (1¼ CUPS) INSTANT
    COUSCOUS (SEE NOTE)
1 TABLESPOON OLIVE OIL
½ TEASPOON SALT
¼ TEASPOON FRESHLY GROUND
    BLACK PEPPER
FINELY GRATED ZEST OF 1 LEMON
310 ML (1¼ CUPS) BOILING WATER
2 TABLESPOONS CHOPPED
    FLAT-LEAF PARSLEY

Heat the olive oil in a large frying pan on a medium heat and fry the onion for about 10 minutes without browning, until soft. Add the garlic and spices and cook for a further 5 minutes. Add the tomatoes, tomato paste, stock and sugar, bring to the boil, then simmer for about 10 minutes until slightly thickened. Season to taste with salt and pepper. Add the fish and simmer on a low heat for 4–5 minutes until just cooked.

To make the couscous, mix the couscous, olive oil, salt, pepper and lemon zest in a bowl. Add the boiling water and stir through. Cover tightly with plastic wrap and set aside for 25 minutes. Uncover, fluff up the couscous with a fork, then mix in the parsley. Serve with the fish.

Serves 4

Note: Some brands of couscous may require a different method of preparation to the one used here. You may prefer to follow the instructions on the packet.

Benjamin David

My parents were born in Rangoon, Burma. They immigrated to Indonesia in the 1930s because it was a difficult time for people of Indian descent to be living in Burma. When the Japanese invaded Indonesia in 1942, I was four. We were put into a POW camp for three years. Luckily my mother was a wonderful cook, and in the camp she was appointed head of the kitchen. I gained my love of cooking from her.

I came to Sydney in 1961 and my parents followed one year later. We were so happy to be together again. When I first came to Australia, I used to write home for cooking instructions, and Mum gladly sent me her recipes. My favourite food of hers was a simple dish of snake beans with chicken. Now every time my wife makes it for me, I am transported right back to Indonesia.

Sunday is my day for cooking, when our extended family come over to our place for brunch. It's become quite a tradition now, and I take great pleasure in cooking for them all.

I remember eating this dish in restaurants in Indonesia, and when I came to Australia I really missed it. Many years ago I asked friends for the recipe, and I started making and adapting it to suit my own taste. This dish reminds me of the time before Australia was home.

FISH SAMBAL

100 G LONG RED MILD CHILLIES, ROUGHLY CHOPPED

1–3 BULLET CHILLIES, TO TASTE (OPTIONAL)

2 TOMATOES, FRESH OR TINNED, PEELED

1 KG BONELESS, SKINLESS FIRM WHITE FISH FILLETS, SUCH AS BLUE EYE TREVALLA OR PERCH

2 TABLESPOONS CANOLA OIL

2 LARGE ONIONS, FINELY CHOPPED

2 TEASPOONS CRUSHED GARLIC

2 TABLESPOONS KECAP MANIS (SWEET SOY SAUCE)

2 KAFFIR LIME LEAVES

1 STALK LEMONGRASS, SMASHED

1 TEASPOON TAMARIND PASTE (OR USE ½ LEMON, JUICED)

Put the chillies and tomatoes into a blender and blend to form a paste. Set aside.

Cut the fish into pieces and lightly salt them. Heat half the oil in a large non-stick wok or frying pan on a high heat. Sear the fish pieces until lightly golden but not cooked through, then remove from the wok.

Fry the onions in the same wok, using a little more oil, until brown. Add the garlic and cook for a further minute before adding the chilli paste, kecap manis, kaffir lime leaves, lemongrass and tamarind. Continue cooking on a medium heat for 20–30 minutes until the mixture has become a rich sauce. When ready to serve, add the fish and simmer for 6 minutes, or until just cooked through. Remove the lemongrass stalk and serve with steamed rice.

Serves 4–6

Daphne Doctor

My late husband, Hans, loved good food and always said that he married me because of my mother's cooking! Originally from Germany, he arrived in South Africa just before the war, and then served in the South African army during World War II. We met in 1947 and married one year later, when I was twenty.

As Hans well recognised, my mother was an excellent cook, but I had no real need to learn to cook while growing up. It wasn't until I married that I found I actually enjoyed cooking, and loved to prepare our meals myself, even though this was really not the norm in those days in Johannesburg. We had four sons, and when they brought their friends home, I enjoyed feeding all of them, too.

Many years later, our family left South Africa and settled in Sydney. Our sons are now all married, with children of their own. They all love to cook and eat well, which I'm sure is something they've inherited. From early on we had Friday nights at our place and still today I often manage to have the family around and cook them dinner. It is one of my greatest joys to nurture my family in this way, and to watch my nine wonderful grandchildren growing up before my eyes.

After spending time with Hans' crowd, I got to know and appreciate German cooking. This greatly influenced what I like to cook today. My husband's favourite Sunday lunch dish was roast duck with red cabbage and apple sauce. This duck recipe originated in a 1985 Evelyn Rose book called The New Jewish Cuisine. *It is now a favourite of my friends, my sons, my brother and all their families, and it is what I have become well known for.*

CRISP GLAZED DUCK

2 FRESH WHOLE DUCKS
4 STALKS PARSLEY, ROUGHLY
   CHOPPED
2 CARROTS, PEELED AND SLICED
2 HEAPED TABLESPOONS BROWN
   SUGAR
2 HEAPED TEASPOONS SALT
100 ML BOILING WATER

Start this recipe the day before. Remove all the fat from inside the ducks, particularly from the parson's nose. Wash the ducks and dry them extremely well. Wrap and stuff the ducks with paper towels and refrigerate overnight, changing the paper towels from time to time. It is vital that the ducks are completely dry.

When you are ready to cook the ducks, preheat the oven to 180°C. You will need a large roasting tin with a rack over it. Remove the paper towels from the ducks, season the cavities well with salt and pepper, and then stuff the cavities with the parsley and carrots.

To make the glaze, mix together the sugar, salt and boiling water until dissolved. Put the ducks, breast side up, on the rack and brush some of the glaze all over them. Place in the oven and roast for 30 minutes, then remove and prick the ducks all over with a sharp fork. Put the rack (and ducks) aside and tip out all the fat and juice in the tin. Return the rack and ducks to the roasting tin, brush with the glaze again and return to the hot oven. Roast for a further 20 minutes. Repeat the steps above (tipping off the juice and glazing the ducks) three times, until you have a total cooking time of about 1 hour 50 minutes, or until the ducks are cooked through and are a deep golden brown.

Remove from the oven and cut each duck into four pieces. Serve with the apple sauce and red cabbage (page 44). If made ahead, reheat quickly in a hot oven until crisp.

Serves 8

My husband loved this simple cabbage dish, as it reminded him of growing up in the old Germany. I got the recipe many years ago from a German friend and it has become a permanent accompaniment to the roast duck.

RED CABBAGE

1 ONION, FINELY SLICED
1 TABLESPOON VEGETABLE OIL
½ RED CABBAGE, VERY FINELY
   SLICED
2 GRANNY SMITH APPLES, PEELED,
   CORED AND VERY FINELY SLICED
55 G (¼ CUP) SUGAR, OR TO TASTE
60 ML (¼ CUP) WHITE VINEGAR,
   OR TO TASTE

In a large saucepan, fry the onion in the oil until soft. Add the cabbage and apples and cook for about 15 minutes, or until soft. Season with salt and then add the sugar and vinegar and taste; there should be a good balance of each. Continue to cook for a further 20–30 minutes until soft. Serve immediately or reheat to serve.

Serves 8

APPLE SAUCE

8 GRANNY SMITH APPLES,
   QUARTERED (NOT PEELED
   OR CORED)
2 TABLESPOONS SUGAR
FINELY GRATED ZEST AND JUICE
   OF 1 LEMON

Cook the apples in a saucepan of boiling water until soft, then drain. Pass the apples through a mouli or sieve to form a purée and to remove the pips and skin. Add the sugar and lemon juice to taste. Refrigerate until ready to serve. Sprinkle with the lemon zest before serving.

Serves 8

The Dons

Sophie Smith

There was always something cooking in Bobba Sophie's kitchen: home-pickled cucumbers, boiled fruitcake or her famous hazenblozen, fried pastry dusted with icing sugar. She loved nothing more than hearing the doorbell ring. Out came the teapot, good china and polished silverware as she welcomed people into her home.

Sophie often reminisced about her parents, the Linskys, who emigrated from Russia to Brisbane. They opened their home each Shabbat to welcome new migrants with a table laden with home-cooked food. They often went on picnics, her father pushing the wooden cart loaded with the samovar, a large brick of ice and their own pickled tomatoes and cucumbers, wine and schnapps. Sophie grew up in this warm, hospitable family and absorbed her passion for food from her parents. Sophie passed away in 2008.

Railea Don

I arrived in Sydney from the USA in 1941 with my parents, Sophie and Harold Smith. My maternal grandmother was an excellent traditional Russian-style cook. I still remember eating her breakfast kreplach, pastry rounds filled with fresh homemade cottage cheese, served with sour cream. My father's mother specialised in gefilte fish, apple pies and cheesecakes.

I loved studying home economics at high school and at sixteen started working at the Gas Company, doing cooking demonstrations in front of an auditorium full of people. In those days we would also visit people's homes and check their oven temperatures by baking a batch of scones in their oven! I then joined the Sydney County Council, teaching young housewives food preparation. When my children were older, I qualified as a teacher and taught at TAFE for over twenty years. It was wonderful when my daughter Melissa joined me there as a teacher — we were quite a team.

Melissa Port

My earliest memory is sitting in the kitchen and watching Mum delicately decorating wedding cakes with the finest of royal icing flowers. There was always a cake in the oven and cucumbers or herring pickling. I grew up tasting minced raw fish to balance the seasonings for gefilte fish, and licking beaters coated in sticky sweet icing. I had no idea I was learning from the best: my mother and grandmother.

While still studying, I worked at Accoutrement cooking school, and then ran my own classes there in chocolate making. Then, in the 1980s, with a keen eye for photography I became a food stylist. Today I run a boutique cooking school, Mia Cucina School of Cookery. I now share the knowledge of past generations with my students and with my own four children, who love nothing more than making hollandaise sauce for the poached eggs, or rolling out homemade pastry for an apple pie. I wonder if they realise they are the next chapter?

Railea

I was given this recipe some years ago by my daughter, Simone. I was taken with its unique method, its combination of exotic ingredients and its delicious flavour. It is now one of my favourites. If you don't keep kosher, serve it with ½ cup labna dolloped around the lamb.

SLOW-ROASTED FRAGRANT SPRING LAMB WITH POMEGRANATE

1 TEASPOON CUMIN SEEDS
2 TEASPOONS CORIANDER SEEDS
2 TEASPOONS SEA SALT
OLIVE OIL
1 LAMB SHOULDER ON THE BONE,
    ABOUT 2.5 KG
250 ML (1 CUP) WATER
½ BUNCH MINT, LEAVES ONLY
2 SPANISH (RED) ONIONS, FINELY
    SLICED INTO RINGS
1 POMEGRANATE, SEEDS REMOVED
HARISSA, TO SERVE
1 LEMON, QUARTERED

Start this recipe the day before. Using a mortar and pestle, grind the cumin seeds, coriander seeds and sea salt together. Rub the olive oil into the lamb, then rub the ground spices into the meat. Place the lamb in a large plastic bag or cover with plastic wrap and refrigerate overnight.

Preheat the oven to 140°C. Remove the lamb from the bag and place into a baking dish. Add the water, cover tightly with foil and roast for 2 hours. Reduce the oven to 110°C and cook for a further 5 hours, removing the foil for the last hour of roasting to crisp the outer skin. Check the lamb at intervals during cooking time to ensure the dish is not completely dry.

Remove from the oven and allow the lamb to cool slightly, then tear the meat in large shards from the bone and spread evenly over a serving platter. Strew with torn mint leaves, onion rings and pomegranate seeds. Serve with the harissa and lemon quarters on the side.

Serves 6–8

Railea

I taught this to so many students over the years at the Sydney County Council. It was a staple recipe and always a favourite. It is known as the '2 4 6 8' recipe as it has 2 eggs, 4 oz butter, 6 oz sugar and 8 oz flour (and ½ cup liquid). I also used this recipe to make hundreds of lamingtons for the annual fete at the Montefiore Home. Every year my kitchen would be filled with thirty slabs of cake, lined up on every work surface possible, ready for covering in masses of dripping chocolate and coconut. People would drop in, roll up their sleeves and all have a turn at dipping and rolling.

LAMINGTONS

CAKE

125 G UNSALTED BUTTER, AT ROOM
  TEMPERATURE
185 G CASTER SUGAR
2 EGGS
250 G (1⅔ CUPS) SELF-RAISING
  FLOUR
125 ML (½ CUP) MILK OR
  ORANGE JUICE

COATING

500 G ICING SUGAR MIXTURE
3 TABLESPOONS COCOA POWDER
1 TABLESPOON UNSALTED BUTTER
250 ML (1 CUP) HOT WATER
250 G SHREDDED OR DESICCATED
  COCONUT

Preheat the oven to 180°C. Line a 28 x 19 x 4 cm lamington tin.

To make the cake, cream the butter and sugar until the sugar is dissolved. Add the eggs one at a time, beating after each addition. Gradually add the flour, alternating with the milk or orange juice. Mix together well, then pour the mixture evenly into the prepared tin. Bake for 30 minutes, or until a skewer inserted into the cake comes out clean. Allow the cake to cool completely, then cut into 4 cm squares, trimming the edges if necessary.

Mix the icing sugar and cocoa together in a bowl. Put the butter into the hot water to melt, and mix into the icing sugar mixture until thick and smooth. Drop the cake squares into the chocolate, ensuring the cake is fully covered, then remove very quickly. Drain the cake on a wire rack for a few seconds. Using a large cooking fork, roll in the coconut.

Makes about 30 small lamingtons

Melissa

I bake this cake in Bobba Sophie's original octagonal tin. In her time, Sophie used to make three dozen orange cakes for the annual Montefiore Home fete, never needing to refer to the recipe. And in a true show of support, Poppa Harold juiced the oranges and lined the cake tins for each and every cake.

SOPHIE'S ORANGE CAKE

CAKE
125 G UNSALTED BUTTER, AT ROOM
    TEMPERATURE
230 G (1 CUP) CASTER SUGAR
2 EGGS
225 G (1½ CUPS) SELF-RAISING
    FLOUR, SIFTED
125 ML (½ CUP) FRESH ORANGE
    JUICE

ICING
1 TABLESPOON UNSALTED BUTTER,
    AT ROOM TEMPERATURE
2 TABLESPOONS ORANGE JUICE
240 G (1½ CUPS) ICING SUGAR
    MIXTURE, SIFTED

Preheat the oven to 180°C. Grease a 20 cm ring cake tin and line with baking paper.

Cream the butter and sugar until light and fluffy. Add the eggs one at a time, beating after each addition, then beat for a further 2 minutes. Gradually add the flour, alternating with the orange juice, and fold into the mixture. Place the mixture into the prepared tin and bake for 30 minutes, or until a skewer inserted into the cake comes out clean. Leave the cake to cool in the tin for 5 minutes before turning out onto a wire rack to cool completely before icing.

To make the icing, cream the butter and then slowly beat in the orange juice and icing sugar until the mixture is smooth and thick. If you prefer a runny icing, add a little more orange juice. Spread the icing over the top of the cooled cake.

Serves 8

June Edelmuth

Cooking fills every part of my life. Although I qualified in Johannesburg as a primary school teacher, my real passion was always food. I ran a cooking school and catering business, and during that time wrote three cookbooks. We had some exciting times, catering for people such as King Goodwill Zwelithini from Swaziland, Nelson Mandela and Tokyo Sexwale. My mother passed on to me the culinary skills that she had learnt from my grandmother, with both Russian and South African influences. Many of the recipes I write have been inspired by the varied ethnic cultures and wonderful restaurants I have visited.

After we immigrated to Sydney, I continued to work in the food industry with my husband, Steve, and now we are partners in Passion8 catering. Because of the long hours I work, I take lots of short cuts when it comes to preparing everyday family meals; fresh, last-minute food has become my forte. I love entertaining, and can never resist buying beautiful platters — they really do enhance the food.

These succulent and slightly spicy livers have been part of my cooking repertoire for many years. Serve them with Portuguese bread rolls or crusty bread for dipping, or as a topping for toasted Italian bread. If you are doubling the recipe, do not double the peri peri oil.

PORTUGUESE PERI PERI CHICKEN LIVERS

2 TABLESPOONS VEGETABLE OIL
500 G CHICKEN LIVERS, CLEANED
60 ML (¼ CUP) PERI PERI OIL
  OR CHILLI OIL
1 LARGE ONION, CHOPPED
1 SMALL CHILLI, SEEDED AND
  CHOPPED
1 CLOVE GARLIC, CRUSHED
½ TEASPOON FINELY GRATED
  FRESH GINGER
125 ML (½ CUP) TOMATO SAUCE
  (KETCHUP)
60 ML (¼ CUP) RED WINE OR PORT
125 ML (½ CUP) WATER
½ TEASPOON CHILLI PASTE
  OR SAUCE
PAPRIKA AND/OR PERI PERI
  POWDER, TO TASTE

Heat the oil in a frying pan and fry the livers on a medium heat for 5 minutes, or until almost cooked through. Be gentle so the livers do not fall apart. Remove from the pan and set aside.

Add the peri peri oil or chilli oil to the pan and fry the onion for 10–15 minutes, or until soft and golden. Add the chilli, garlic and ginger and fry for a further minute, then add the tomato sauce, wine, water and chilli paste. Stir in the paprika and/or peri peri powder and season with salt and pepper to taste. Bring to the boil, then reduce the heat and simmer for 10 minutes until the flavours have combined.

Add the livers to the onion mixture and cook for a further 5–10 minutes, or until the sauce has thickened. Check the spices and season to taste. Serve warm or at room temperature. This recipe can be made the day before and reheated.

Serves 6–8 as a starter

Janice Einfeld

Australia was always home for Janice, her parents both immigrating here from Europe when they were children. Dover Heights was a fabulous place to grow up, with many of her friends living just around the corner and across the road.

She married Graham, also a Sydneysider, and before starting a family they lived in Canada. Janice hadn't spent a lot of time in the kitchen as a young girl, so when she arrived in Toronto she realised she had no mother or mother-in-law nearby to teach her the tricks of the trade. Janice figured she had better learn how to cook or they would all go hungry! The local butcher took her under his wing, kindly telling her that if she worked out what they wanted to eat every week, he would advise her which cut of meat to buy and what to do with it.

Once they moved back to Sydney and had a family of their own, Janice took a special interest in gluten-free baking and made all sorts of biscuits and cakes without flour. She did all her own baking and enjoyed it very much, as did her family. Janice sadly passed away in 2012.

Janice made this recipe for over 30 years, ever since she got it from her sister's mother-in-law. Among her family and friends it was known as 'Nicey's date slice', and was an expected and constant part of her baking repertoire. If a friend was celebrating a simcha — *whether it was a newborn baby or a birthday — Janice would make a batch and drop it over. It has always been the perfect sweet treat with a cup of coffee in the afternoon. Nicey's slice will always be a beautiful reminder of an inspirational and special woman who touched the lives of many.*

NICEY'S DATE SLICE

125 G UNSALTED BUTTER
250 G (1⅓ CUPS) BROWN SUGAR
1 EGG, BEATEN
150 G (1 CUP) SELF-RAISING FLOUR
250 G (1½ CUPS) CHOPPED DRIED
  DATES

Preheat the oven to 180°C. Line a 25 x 18 cm lamington tin.

Combine the butter and sugar in a saucepan on a medium–high heat for a few minutes, stirring constantly until dissolved and melted. Remove from the heat, pour the melted butter mixture into a large bowl and allow to cool slightly. When cool, add the egg and stir well, then add the flour, stir again, and finally, the dates. Mix together with a wooden or metal spoon.

Place the date mixture into the prepared tin and bake for 15–20 minutes. Cut into slices when cool. Store in an airtight container for a week – if it lasts that long!

Makes about 20 pieces

Haviva Elais

I remember with great nostalgia my childhood in India, and the intoxicating smell of spices filling the night air. Mummy cooked the food of her country so well — curry, dahl and many other such dishes. When she moved to London, she introduced these dishes to the many English Jews in her neighbourhood who, along with her own eight children, loved her food.

My mother used to say that she cooked with love, which is why I think her food tasted so good. I followed her ways, and started to cook for my four daughters with just as much love. I do try to cook as many of her dishes as possible, to help keep her memory alive. This way, she will always be with us.

Indian curry utilises many of the traditional Indian spices and, in my opinion, is the best curry in the world, but I always thought it was funny that curries are eaten so often in such a hot country! Nobody really taught me how to cook this dish; I just experimented with different spice combinations after watching my mother for many years. I made it badly at first, but I've had forty years to perfect it!

THE ELAIS FAMILY ORIGINAL CURRY

2 TABLESPOONS VEGETABLE OIL
3 ONIONS, FINELY CHOPPED
3 CLOVES GARLIC, CRUSHED
1 TEASPOON GRATED FRESH
  GINGER
3 TEASPOONS CURRY POWDER
1 TEASPOON GROUND CUMIN
1 TEASPOON GROUND CORIANDER
1 TABLESPOON VINDALOO PASTE
1 LARGE TOMATO, BLANCHED (OR
  MICROWAVED FOR 1½ MINUTES),
  PEELED AND CHOPPED
250 ML (1 CUP) WATER
1.5–2 KG CHICKEN, LAMB OR
  STEWING BEEF (OFF THE BONE),
  CUT INTO LARGE CUBES
3 POTATOES, PEELED AND CUT
  INTO SMALL CHUNKS

Heat the oil in a large frying pan and gently fry the onions on a medium heat for about 10 minutes, or until soft. Add the garlic and ginger and cook for 2 minutes, stirring, then add the curry powder, cumin, coriander and vindaloo paste. Cook through for several minutes. Add the tomato and about 125 ml (½ cup) of the water and cook for a few minutes, stirring, then add the meat and cook for a further 5 minutes.

Add the remaining water to the pan. Cover the pan with the lid and continue to simmer until cooked. The chicken will take around 20–30 minutes, the lamb and beef about 1½–2 hours. If cooking chicken, add the potatoes just after you have added the chicken, otherwise add them when 40 minutes of cooking time remains.

Serves 6–8

Natanya Eskin

Growing up in a traditional Jewish home meant being constantly surrounded by food. In some of my earliest memories of Mum I can see her with a wooden spoon in her hand, her faithful Kenwood mixmaster beside her, whirring, beating and whisking. Birthday cakes were always home-baked and always the same: a light butter cake iced in rich dark chocolate with a cream birthday message piped on top.

Nana Betty, my dad's mother, was from Harbin, China, of Russian heritage. Her language was food and feeding us was her only means of communication. My two elder brothers and I were always shouting 'no more' in frustration, but it didn't help; she kept on feeding us until we were too stuffed to argue.

She cooked many wonderful dishes, including a unique gefilte fish. Her secret was to cook the brown onion skins in the stock, which gave it a darker than usual colour, and then to mince the fish three times over for a wonderfully smooth texture. I have never seen or tasted a similar version. On special occasions she would produce an almond and coffee cake with coffee cream icing piped all over the top, piled up like twisted spaghetti. How I loved that!

Baking started out as a hobby for me, but over the years it's become a part-time profession and quite a fascination. Even though Nana Betty passed away many years ago, she was a wonderful inspiration to me, and I like to think I'm following in her footsteps a little. I now experience the same joy that she did when I proudly present my children with a freshly baked cake, and watch their faces light up, just like mine used to.

Nana Betty's specialty was her fish pie, a wonderful relic from her Russian and Chinese heritage, made with salmon, vermicelli noodles and onions, encased in the flakiest sour cream pastry. It always sat proudly in the centre of the table at family gatherings. Only now do I understand the hours and hours that Nana spent in the kitchen, preparing and cooking for her family, and the joy she experienced from watching us devour the fruits of her labour.

BETTY'S FISH PIE

PASTRY

600 G (4 CUPS) SELF-RAISING
   FLOUR
250 G COLD BUTTER, CHOPPED
½ TEASPOON SALT
2 EGGS, BEATEN
150 G SOUR CREAM
3 TEASPOONS CASTER SUGAR

FILLING

120 G FINE VERMICELLI NOODLES
8 LARGE ONIONS, COARSELY
   CHOPPED
120 ML VEGETABLE OIL
6 HARD-BOILED EGGS, COARSELY
   CHOPPED
1 KG SKINLESS SALMON FILLETS,
   POACHED (SEE NOTE) AND
   FLAKED, OR 800 G TIN RED
   SALMON, DRAINED AND
   BROKEN UP
1 EGG, BEATEN, FOR GLAZING

Preheat the oven to 170°C. Grease a 34 x 22 x 5 cm baking tin.

To make the pastry, put the flour, butter and salt in a food processor and process until it forms fine crumbs. Add the eggs, sour cream and sugar and process until the mixture just comes together. Remove to a floured surface and knead gently until a soft dough is formed.

Divide the dough into two pieces (two-thirds and one-third pieces). Roll out the bigger piece on a floured board to fit the base and sides of the tin. Roll out the small piece large enough to make a top for the pie.

To make the filling, soak the noodles in boiling water for 15 minutes, then drain and cool. Meanwhile, fry the onions in the oil over a low heat for 15 minutes, or until soft and golden brown. Season generously with salt and pepper to taste. Gently combine the hard-boiled eggs and salmon and season very generously with salt and pepper.

Assemble the filling in the pastry-lined tin in layers of onions, noodles, egg and salmon, noodles and, lastly, onions. Top with the pastry lid, seal the edges and brush with the beaten egg. Make two small holes in the pie top to allow steam to escape. Bake for 45 minutes, or until golden brown, then remove from the oven and allow to cool a little. Serve at room temperature with sour cream.

Serves 16

Note: To poach the salmon, put 500 ml (2 cups) chicken or vegetable stock in a wide pan with 1 chopped carrot, 1 chopped onion, 1 tablespoon salt, 1 teaspoon pepper and a few sprigs parsley. Bring to the boil, then add the salmon, in one layer if possible. Remove the pan from the heat, cover and set aside to poach for 10 minutes.

My maternal grandmother, Sarah, was almost 101 when she passed away. Many, many years ago, Nana Betty gave Sarah this recipe for lokshen kugel, *a sweet noodle pudding. She was always amazed at what a wonderful cook Betty was and how well she managed out of a tiny kitchen, without the use of any modern utensils. Sarah made this dish so often, eventually it became hers and not Betty's.*

MY GRANDMOTHER SARAH'S LOKSHEN KUGEL

250 G WIDE EGG NOODLES
   (LOKSHEN)
3 EGGS, SEPARATED
80 G (⅓ CUP) CASTER SUGAR
500 G (2 CUPS) RICOTTA CHEESE
160 G (1 CUP) SULTANAS
1 LARGE GRANNY SMITH APPLE,
   PEELED AND GRATED
100 G UNSALTED BUTTER, MELTED
CINNAMON SUGAR, FOR
   SPRINKLING

Preheat the oven to 180°C. Grease a 25 x 20 cm baking dish.

Cook the noodles in a large saucepan of boiling salted water until just cooked. Drain and rinse with cold water.

Whisk the egg whites until stiff peaks form. In a separate large bowl, beat together the egg yolks and sugar until light. Beat in the ricotta until well combined, then add the sultanas and apple and mix well. Mix in the noodles and melted butter, then gently fold through the egg whites.

Place the mixture in the baking dish and sprinkle with the cinnamon sugar. Bake for 50–60 minutes, or until the top is golden and a little crisp. Serve warm or at room temperature.

Serves 12

The Fayn sisters

Sara Robenstone

Soon after announcing their engagement, my parents left Poland in the 1920s to start a new life in Melbourne. They married and settled in North Carlton and had four children: me, my sisters Raie and Shirley, and my brother, Morrie.

I used to help Mum at home but never really took the time or interest to learn to cook. So when I married Syd in 1950, my father was greatly concerned that my poor husband might starve to death! Taking inspiration from my mother (who had passed away by that time) and through much trial and error, I managed to become an accomplished cook. Many years on, cooking is one of my most enjoyable pastimes and we thrive on our large family gatherings where food most often takes centre stage.

Raie Rosenberg

Raie was sixteen when their father moved the family (except for newly married Sara) to Sydney, and had already begun to develop a strong interest in food and cooking. She happily settled into life in a new city, married Ron and started a family of her own.

When Raie and Ron opened Aunty Raie's Deli in Woollahra in the eighties, she lovingly cooked all the house dishes herself. Her specialties included chopped liver, egg and onion, a huge variety of frittatas and, of course, her meatloaf. With her chatty personality and sense of humour, she adored the local customers and thrived on the camaraderie that existed in the area. Raie passed away in 1997. She is remembered not only for her exceptional cooking but also for being an integral Woollahra village personality.

Raie's best-known specialty was her incredible meatloaf. She sold it across Sydney to many cafes and sandwich bars, and customers would queue outside her deli at lunch time to buy one of her famous meatloaf sandwiches.

AUNTY RAIE'S MEATLOAF

MEATLOAF

1 KG BEEF TOPSIDE MINCE
  (OR CHICKEN AND VEAL)
1 BROWN ONION, GRATED
1 CARROT, PEELED AND GRATED
1 EGG, BEATEN
80 G (1 CUP) FRESH BREADCRUMBS
  (SEE NOTE)
2 CLOVES GARLIC, CRUSHED
2 TABLESPOONS TOMATO SAUCE
  (KETCHUP)
2–3 TABLESPOONS
  WORCESTERSHIRE SAUCE
1 HANDFUL CHOPPED PARSLEY

GLAZE

80 ML (⅓ CUP) TOMATO SAUCE
  (KETCHUP)
80 ML (⅓ CUP) WORCESTERSHIRE
  SAUCE
60 G (⅓ CUP) BROWN SUGAR
80 ML (⅓ CUP) WATER

Place all the ingredients for the meatloaf into a large bowl and mix together with your hands. Season generously with salt and pepper and allow to rest for several hours in the fridge.

Preheat the oven to 180°C. Lightly grease a large roasting tin. With wet hands, mould the meatloaf mixture into a long log and place it in the tin. The thinner (and longer) the log, the more delicious crust you will have. If you prefer, you can make two smaller logs.

Mix together the ingredients for the glaze and pour it over the meatloaf. Place the tin in the oven and cook for 1 hour, basting often, until glazed and brown.

Serves 8

Note: To make fresh breadcrumbs, remove the crusts from good-quality white bread or sourdough and process until fine crumbs are formed.

Sara first made this for her husband's fiftieth birthday. She had wanted to make American pastrami and not being able to find a recipe, decided to experiment — she's been making this version for Rosh Hashanah and Yom Kippur for over thirty years since. Her pickled brisket rose to even greater fame in the early nineties when she made it for her son Peter, owner of Bon Cafe in Toorak. She made seven every week, which were then used for the cafe's best-selling sandwich, 'Sara's Brisket', served on rye bread with pickled cucumbers and a spoonful of the caramelised onions from the pan.

SARA'S PICKLED BRISKET

1 PICKLED (CORNED) BEEF BRISKET
250 ML (1 CUP) WHITE VINEGAR
220 G (1 CUP) RAW OR WHITE
   SUGAR
9 BAY LEAVES
1 SMALL HANDFUL BLACK
   PEPPERCORNS
4 CLOVES GARLIC, CRUSHED
4 LARGE BROWN ONIONS, HALVED
   AND SLICED
250–300 G HONEY
2 TABLESPOONS VEGETABLE OIL

If possible, start this recipe the day before. Put the brisket in a large saucepan and cover with water. Add the vinegar and sugar, then bring to the boil, skimming any scum off the surface. Taste to check you have an equal and strong flavour of both vinegar and sugar, and adjust if necessary. Add the bay leaves and peppercorns. Cover the pan with a lid and simmer rapidly for about 2 hours, or until fork-tender.

Drain and place the brisket in a non-stick roasting tin. Rub the garlic over the meat while it is still warm, and allow to cool a little before refrigerating overnight, if possible.

When ready to cook, preheat the oven to 175°C. Cover the meat with the sliced onions and pour over the honey. Drizzle with the oil. Roast, uncovered, for about 45 minutes, basting frequently, until the meat is tender and the onions are golden.

Slice thickly across the grain and serve warm with mashed potatoes and cabbage, or in a sandwich on fresh rye bread with mustard, pickled cucumber and coleslaw.

A 2 kg brisket will serve 10–12, with leftovers for sandwiches

Sharen Fink

I grew up surrounded by an army of women who introduced me to the pleasure of cooking for others. My greatest inspiration was, and still is, my Australian-born grandmother, Buba Nita. She and my mum are both wonderful cooks. I marvel at how Buba would always be up late cooking her delicious salmon patties and, to my grandfather's delight, an apple tart handed down from her mother-in-law.

After university, my interests leaned towards the food industry. I started selling cakes and dabbling in catering. I worked in food marketing, then further cemented my food knowledge by undertaking a year-long intensive cooking course in Paris.

It was after a call from my uncle Leon (owner of Quay restaurant in Sydney), asking me to come and work for him as operations manager, that I packed up and moved to Sydney. I worked at Quay for two years and then met Simon, whom I married. We settled back in Melbourne and I've now taken a pause in my food career, but made a wonderful start to our family career.

Some say this salad dates back to the Book of Exodus, but I have made a more 'modern' version by using quinoa instead of the traditional burghul. The key to this salad is to use a good olive oil and quality sea salt.

QUINOA TABBOULEH

200 G (1 CUP) QUINOA
500 ML (2 CUPS) WATER
PINCH OF SALT
2 BUNCHES FLAT-LEAF PARSLEY,
    CHOPPED
½ BUNCH MINT, CHOPPED
6 RIPE TOMATOES, SEEDED AND
    DICED
4 LEBANESE CUCUMBERS, SEEDED
    AND DICED
1 BUNCH SPRING ONIONS, SLICED
½ TEASPOON ALLSPICE
JUICE OF 1 LEMON
100 ML GOOD-QUALITY OLIVE OIL
BABY COS LETTUCE, SEPARATED
    INTO LEAVES, TO SERVE

To prepare the quinoa, first rinse well with cold water and drain. Place the quinoa in a saucepan with the water and salt. Bring to the boil, stir, and then simmer on a medium heat for about 12 minutes, or until all the water is absorbed. Rinse under cold water and drain well. It is very important the quinoa is dry.

In a bowl, toss together the parsley, mint, tomatoes, cucumbers and spring onions. Add the quinoa.

Mix the allspice and lemon juice in a bowl. Season with sea salt and freshly ground black pepper, then whisk in the olive oil. Taste for seasoning. Pour the dressing over the tabbouleh and toss carefully. Season again with salt and pepper, then place in the fridge for an hour or so to give the flavours time to develop. Tabbouleh is traditionally served in a shallow, wide dish, garnished with baby cos leaves. The leaves are used as a scoop; close the leaf together lengthways in your hand and eat.

Serves 8–10

In my family, nothing quite brings the same enjoyment from around the table as Buba's eggplant. This recipe is a true family heirloom — it's full of flavour … and love. She makes several every Friday, for herself and to put in all of our fridges. This recipe involves quite a bit of preparation, but it's ideal for making in advance as it benefits from being left overnight for the flavours to develop. Serve at room temperature on toast, as a mezze or as an accompaniment to white fish or lamb.

BUBA'S EGGPLANT

2 LARGE EGGPLANTS
250 ML (1 CUP) OLIVE OIL

TOMATO SAUCE
60 ML (¼ CUP) OLIVE OIL
1 SMALL ONION, CHOPPED INTO
   SMALL DICE
8 CLOVES GARLIC, CRUSHED
1 TABLESPOON TOMATO PASTE
2 x 400 G TINS DICED TOMATOES

Cut the eggplant into 8 mm thick slices. Lay the slices on paper towel and sprinkle both sides with salt. Leave for 10 minutes, then wipe off any excess moisture with paper towel.

Meanwhile, to make the tomato sauce, heat the olive oil in a saucepan on a medium heat. Add the onion and cook for 5 minutes until soft and translucent. Add the garlic and cook slowly for a further 10 minutes, stirring from time to time. Add the tomato paste and cook for 2 minutes, then add the tomatoes and season to taste with salt and freshly ground black pepper. Simmer for at least 30 minutes, or until a rich sauce forms. Check the seasoning and set aside.

Heat the olive oil in a large frying pan and shallow-fry the eggplant in batches for a few minutes on each side until just golden. Drain on paper towel.

Preheat the oven to 180°C. Grease a shallow 20 x 22 cm ovenproof dish. To assemble, spoon one-third of the tomato sauce into the dish. Add a single layer of eggplant and sprinkle with salt and pepper. Repeat the process, finishing with a scant covering of tomato sauce. Bake for 45 minutes until a crust has formed. Cool slightly and spoon off any excess oil, leaving a thin covering of oil to protect the eggplant. Allow to cool. Store in the fridge but bring to room temperature to serve.

Serves 6–8 as a side dish

Variations: If desired, add torn basil leaves over the eggplant slices. For added richness, add thin slices of buffalo mozzarella or freshly grated parmesan cheese (or both) over the eggplant.

Renee Glass

I come from a long line of bakers and cooks, starting with my Lithuanian grandparents who owned a bakery back in the old country. My childhood in South Africa was always filled with the enticing and memorable smells of freshly baked goods. In the early eighties when my granny was still alive, I sat her down and wrote out all of her recipes, making sure she told me the exact quantities she used. Now when I make one of her cakes, I think, 'Well, I've invited my Boba for tea.'

These lovely and slightly unusual sugary biscuits come from an aunt of mine, whom I adore. They are so quick to make; I can whip up a batch if people drop by unexpectedly.

GINGER SNAPS

230 G (1 CUP) CASTER SUGAR

1 EGG, BEATEN

300 G (2 CUPS) PLAIN FLOUR

1 TABLESPOON GROUND GINGER

1 TABLESPOON GROUND
   CINNAMON

2 TEASPOONS BICARBONATE
   OF SODA

140 G UNSALTED BUTTER, MELTED
   AND COOLED A LITTLE

2 TABLESPOONS GOLDEN SYRUP

PINCH OF SALT

WHITE SUGAR (NOT CASTER),
   FOR DIPPING

Preheat the oven to 180°C. Line two baking trays.

Put all the ingredients, except the sugar for dipping, into a food processor and process just until a dough is formed. Roll the dough into walnut-sized balls and dip the top into the sugar. Place them 5 cm apart on the prepared trays. Bake for 12 minutes, or until golden brown. Cool a little on the trays, then transfer to a wire rack.

Makes about 35

This recipe comes from my mum and is truly a family favourite. I created the topping and added it to the recipe, so it becomes a kind of upside-down cake. If serving as a dessert, add extra butter to the topping, so the caramel runs down the cake.

GINGER CAKE

2 TEASPOONS BICARBONATE
   OF SODA
60 ML (¼ CUP) WARM WATER
185 ML (¾ CUP) COLD WATER
230 G (1 CUP) CASTER SUGAR
250 ML (1 CUP) VEGETABLE OIL
350 G (1 CUP) GOLDEN SYRUP
   (SEE NOTE)
3 EGGS
1 TABLESPOON GROUND GINGER
2 TEASPOONS GROUND CINNAMON
2 TEASPOONS MIXED SPICE
450 G (3 CUPS) PLAIN FLOUR

TOPPING (OPTIONAL)
100 G UNSALTED BUTTER
110 G (½ CUP FIRMLY PACKED)
   BROWN SUGAR
150 G (1½ CUPS) PECANS
1 APPLE, PEELED, CORED
   AND SLICED

Preheat the oven to 180°C. Grease a 26 cm ring or bundt tin very well.

To make the topping, melt the butter in a saucepan. As soon as it is melted, add the sugar and pecans and mix well, stirring only until the sugar is dissolved. Add the apple and stir through, then pour the sauce into the prepared tin.

To make the cake, dissolve the bicarbonate of soda in the warm water and then add the cold water. Mix all the ingredients together, including the bicarbonate and water, in an electric mixer. Pour the batter into the tin and bake for 1 hour, or until a skewer inserted into the cake comes out clean. Allow to cool for 5 minutes before turning out onto a wire rack.

Serves 12

Note: If you measure the golden syrup after you have measured the oil and use the same measuring cup, the golden syrup will be easier to pour out of the cup.

Lisa Goldberg

I sometimes imagine that I am living in the wrong century and in the wrong place. I dream of stories of my late grandmother, Bubba Sheindel, in Poland. My father describes her cellar as a treasure trove of culinary delights and tantalising aromas, bursting with barrels of her freshly pickled cucumbers, vats of pickled cabbage, apples and tomatoes, of schmaltz and pickled herrings, and preserved fruits and jams. I dream of her cholent, fried fish and cabbage rolls, the likes of which I will never taste, and of her cheesecake, strudel, freshly baked challah and platzallah (onion bread).

She rolled the thinnest pastry for the most perfect apple strudel (or, as my mother says, 'shtroodel'), without a cookbook in sight. Many years later, my mother asked her for the recipe, which of course had never been written down. So my mother stood in the kitchen with a measuring cup and scales and measured and weighed every pinch, spoon and glass of sugar, flour and butter before it went into the mix. This was the only time Bubba's strudel didn't work! The recipe is now long gone, but the story inspired me to want to record our family's recipes, to ensure that at least some of them are passed on to the next generation.

I moved from Melbourne to Sydney for love in the late eighties, and have now made it home with my husband, Danny, and our four children. Our lives revolve somewhat obsessively around food. We plan trips around restaurant visits, tours around gourmet food stores, and shopping around farmers' markets. We photograph it and share; we talk about it and compare; we love eating out and eating in. But more than anything, I just love standing in the kitchen and cooking.

Egg and onion has been part of my parents' Shabbat dinner for as long as I can remember and it is now part of mine. It makes me smile to think how Mum always served a scoop of egg and onion (using an ice-cream scoop!) on a piece of lettuce on each plate. We were taught the recipe by our wonderful Greek housekeeper, Pat, who had learnt the recipe from my grandmother and aunts.

EGG AND ONION

3 BROWN ONIONS, DICED
185 ML (¾ CUP) VEGETABLE OIL
12 EGGS

Put the onions and oil in a large frying pan and fry for about 20 minutes, or until golden brown and very soft. Meanwhile, boil the eggs for 8–10 minutes until hard-boiled. Remove the pan from the heat, drain and then cover the eggs with cold water. When just cool enough to handle, peel the eggs and grate into a large bowl using the coarse side of a grater.

Spoon the onions onto the egg, leaving most of the oil in the pan. Season generously with salt and pepper, and combine the onions and egg with your hands or a wooden spoon, tasting as you go. If too dry, add a little oil from the pan. The mixture should stick together if pressed with your hand, but should not be overly oily.

Cover with plastic wrap until ready to serve, pressing the wrap onto the surface of the egg and onion so it doesn't dry out. Keep at room temperature and serve with challah (page 263) or bagels.

Serves 12 as a starter

Mum's version of brisket uses a young 'calf brisket' (actually a small veal breast on the bone), and is baked and lovingly basted for hours in lots of fried onions. The meat is incredibly succulent, with large bones that are perfect for chewing on. Mum taught me this years ago, and she was taught by her mother, who was taught by her mother in Bialystok, Poland.

PAULA'S CALF BRISKET

4 BROWN ONIONS, COARSELY
   CHOPPED
80 ML (⅓ CUP) VEGETABLE OIL
1 WHOLE BABY CALF BRISKET
   (1.5–2 KG veal breast on
   THE BONE)
2 TABLESPOONS DRIED ONION
   FLAKES
2 TEASPOONS SALT
250 ML (1 CUP) WATER

Preheat the oven to 180°C. Fry the onions in the oil for about 10 minutes, or until lightly brown. Spread the onions over both sides of the brisket and sprinkle with the onion flakes and salt.

Put the brisket, bone side up, in a large baking dish. Add 125 ml (½ cup) of the water and cover tightly with foil. Bake for 2 hours. Remove the foil, turn the brisket over and return the onions to the top of the brisket. Baste with the pan juices, then add the remaining water to the dish. Bake for 1–1½ hours, uncovered, basting every 30 minutes, adding more water as necessary so the bottom of the dish is not dry. Cut into two or three bone portions to serve. This dish reheats well.

Serves 4

Every year that my mother makes this at Passover (for almost fifty guests) it is a little different — some years a little overcooked and deliciously crunchy, other years softer and oilier with just a little crunch around the edges.

ULNYIK (POLISH POTATO CAKE)

250 ML (1 CUP) VEGETABLE OIL
12 PONTIAC POTATOES, PEELED
   AND GRATED (4 HEAPED CUPS)
2 EGGS, BEATEN
2 ONIONS, GRATED
90 G (⅔ CUP) FINE MATZO MEAL
   (OR FLOUR)
1–2 TEASPOONS SALT
½ TEASPOON PEPPER

Preheat the oven to 200°C. Pour the oil into a large deep baking dish (about 40 x 30 cm) and place in the oven to heat.

Squeeze the grated potatoes with your hands until dry. Place in a bowl with the eggs, onions and matzo meal and mix together. Season to taste with the salt and pepper. Carefully remove the hot baking dish from the oven and spoon the mixture into the oil, spreading it out to cover the base. Bake for 1 hour 15 minutes until golden. Allow to cool, then cut into large squares. Reheat in a 200°C oven until piping hot, brown and sizzling.

Serves 12

This recipe came from Lorraine Godsmark (of Rockpool and Yellow Bistro fame), one of Australia's top pastry chefs and also a great teacher. Over the years I have simplified her recipe to make it a little easier. The end result is spectacular, even more so if you increase the quantities and make it in a huge wide vase or glass bowl. It is important to serve it in glass so you can see each of the layers.

PEACH, MASCARPONE AND RASPBERRY TRIFLE

PRALINE
200 G GLUCOSE SYRUP
250 G SUGAR
200 G FLAKED ALMONDS, WARMED

MASCARPONE
3 EGGS, SEPARATED
55 G (¼ CUP) SUGAR
500 G MASCARPONE

RASPBERRY PURÉE
500 G FRESH OR FROZEN
    RASPBERRIES
40 G (¼ CUP) ICING SUGAR

8 YELLOW SLIPSTONE PEACHES
110 G (½ CUP FIRMLY PACKED)
    BROWN SUGAR
1 LARGE SPONGE CAKE (READY-
    MADE OR LAMINGTON SPONGE
    CAKE, PAGE 48), CUT INTO 1 CM
    SLICES OR CUT TO FIT YOUR DISH
2 PUNNETS FRESH RASPBERRIES
    OR 500 G FROZEN RASPBERRIES,
    FOR GARNISH

To make the praline, melt the glucose in a large saucepan and gradually add the sugar, stirring. Cook until it is a deep toffee colour, then quickly stir in the almonds. Pour onto an oiled board or work surface, cover with baking paper and press down with a rolling pin to flatten. When cool, reserve a few shards for decoration, and roughly crush the remainder. Freeze the praline until ready to use. This can be made days ahead.

For the mascarpone, whisk the egg whites with a spoonful of the sugar until stiff. Set aside. Whisk the egg yolks and remaining sugar until creamy. Whisk the mascarpone into the yolk mixture, then gently fold the egg whites into the mascarpone mixture. Refrigerate until ready to use.

To make the raspberry purée, put the raspberries in a blender with enough icing sugar to taste, and purée. Set aside.

Preheat the oven to 200°C. Cut the peaches in half and remove the stones. Place the peaches in a baking dish, cut side up, sprinkle with the brown sugar and bake for 20 minutes, or until soft. Remove from the oven. Remove the skin if you wish, and set aside.

To assemble the trifle you will need a wide glass dish or vase. Layer each ingredient in the dish starting with the cake slices, then the peach halves (drizzling over any juice from the baking dish), then enough mascarpone to cover by about 1 cm, the roughly crushed praline, whole raspberries and the raspberry purée. Repeat until all the ingredients are used. Garnish with the praline shards and berries. Refrigerate for at least 6 hours before serving.

Serves 10–12

Paulette Goldberg

I have a great love of life and a strong sense of family and Jewish tradition, probably because of my experiences as a child kept in hiding during the war. I was born in Paris to Polish parents, but was orphaned by the early age of three. After the war, with the assistance of the Jewish Agency, my sister and I were sent to Brisbane; our brother was already there. We had the wonderful opportunity to leave the past behind and start a new life in Australia.

I was fifteen when I moved to Melbourne. Some years later I met and married Joseph and we had two children to complete our family. I worked for many years as a dressmaker and businesswoman, then Joseph and I decided to move to Sydney in 2005. Our daughter, Michalle, had married a Sydney boy and we wanted to be part of their lives, as well as those of our three wonderful grandchildren. Living in Sydney also means we're closer to our son, Michael, in Byron Bay.

Sadly my husband has now passed away, but I still love being part of the Sydney community and truly delight in watching our grandchildren grow up.

Michalle and I still laugh about the pickles. As a full-time working mother I always made sure the fridge was filled with jars and food with long use-by dates, and always kept a good stock of pickled cucumbers, which I bought by the boxload. For many years I volunteered at the Holocaust Centre in Melbourne, and we would all bring in food to share, and swap recipes with each other. This recipe was given to me then. It is so simple — you will never need to buy another jar again.

MELBOURNE-STYLE PICKLED CUCUMBERS

80 G (¼ CUP) SALT

250 ML (1 CUP) BOILING WATER

24 FRESH GHERKINS (PICKLING
    CUCUMBERS), ALL THE SAME
    SIZE (8–10 CM IN LENGTH)

1 SMALL BUNCH DILL, WASHED,
    BOTTOM STALKS REMOVED

6 CLOVES GARLIC, PEELED

5 RED BIRD'S EYE CHILLIES,
    WASHED

2 SLICES RYE BREAD

You will need a 2 litre (8 cup) wide-mouthed jar or earthenware container. The mouth of the jar needs to be large enough for you to put your hand in.

Make a salt water solution by mixing the salt with the boiling water to dissolve. Add cold water to make 1.5 litres (6 cups) salt water.

Wash the cucumbers in cold water and pat dry. In the bottom of the jar, place 6 dill fronds, 3 cloves garlic and 2 chillies. Place about half the cucumbers in the jar, arranging them vertically, making sure they are a very tight fit. Try to match up sizes and shapes so there is as little air as possible. It is important that you have packed them very tightly – if you were to turn the jar upside down at this stage, the cucumbers should not move.

On top of the first layer of cucumbers, put 6–8 dill fronds, 3 cloves garlic, 3 chillies and then another very tight layer of cucumbers. Top with 6 dill fronds, then fill the jar with salt water to the rim. You will use around 1 litre (4 cups) of salt water.

Trim the bread so it is just bigger than the mouth of the jar, and use the bread to seal the top of the jar, being careful that it stays in one piece. Place the second slice on top, pressing gently into the jar. Add a little more salt water, which will seep through the bread and fill any air bubbles underneath. Cover with the lid.

Leave to pickle for 7–9 days in a cool, dark place. The jar needs to stand in a deep dish, as juice might leak. The cucumbers are almost ready when they change from bright green to dark green. Wait a few more days before opening the jar. Once the jar is opened, the pickling ceases and the dill, garlic and chillies can be removed if you desire. Store the pickles in the pickling liquid in the same jar in the fridge. Keeps for months.

Talia Goldberg

Talia was passionate about the country of her birth, Israel, participating in its 1948 War of Independence as a member of the Palmach. Born in Rehovot in 1930, her family had roots in Palestine. In 1953 she met David, an Australian doctor, also with Israeli roots, who was visiting Israel with his father. They married, sadly farewelled Israel and relocated to Sydney, via England. In London, Talia spent a lot of time with her aunt Rosie, an excellent cook, who taught her so much about cooking and all things food.

Talia devoured cookbooks and food magazines, attended cooking classes, and loved dining with David at Sydney's best restaurants. If there was a dish she really liked, she boldly asked the chef for the recipe, then practised and perfected the dish at home. They travelled the world, and eating and drinking was a most important part of their journey.

While she enjoyed teaching Hebrew and learning Italian, her real pleasure came from cooking for and nurturing her husband and two sons, and then later, her daughters-in-law and seven grandchildren. Now passed on, she has left her family the indelible memory of her Friday night culinary experiences — always delicious and creative gourmet food.

Talia got this salmon recipe many years ago from her friend Moira Lipman, and made it for many years, particularly during the hot summer months. She would prepare the salmon in the afternoon, so when her hungry grandchildren arrived she could concentrate on feeding them her legendary chicken schnitzels, rather than standing at the stove.

SALMON WITH A SESAME AND GINGER CRUST

1 HEAPED TABLESPOON GRATED
    FRESH GINGER
2 CLOVES GARLIC, CRUSHED
60 ML (¼ CUP) SHERRY
2 TEASPOONS SESAME OIL
2 TABLESPOONS SESAME SEEDS
1 BUNCH SPRING ONIONS
    (12 STEMS), FINELY SLICED
½ TEASPOON SEA SALT, OR
    TO TASTE
4 SALMON FILLETS, SKINNED
    AND BONED

Preheat the oven's top grill to its maximum temperature. Cover a flat oven tray with foil.

Mix the ginger and garlic in a bowl, then add the sherry, sesame oil, sesame seeds, spring onions and sea salt and stir to combine. Place the salmon fillets on the tray and spoon a thick layer of the sesame mixture on top. You may cook this immediately or cover and set aside (refrigerate if need be) until you wish to cook it – up to 24 hours.

Place the tray under the hot grill (on the second to top shelf) for 7–10 minutes, or until the salmon is still rare in the middle and the spring onions have blackened. Remove from the oven and set aside. Serve at room temperature.

Serves 4

CABBAGE SALAD

55 G (¼ CUP) SUGAR
125 ML (½ CUP) WHITE VINEGAR
60 ML (¼ CUP) VEGETABLE OIL
2 TABLESPOONS SOY SAUCE
½ SMALL SAVOY OR ½ RED
    CABBAGE (OR A MIXTURE),
    FINELY SHREDDED
80 G (½ CUP) WHOLE ROASTED
    ALMONDS, ROUGHLY CHOPPED
1 HEAPED TABLESPOON TOASTED
    SESAME SEEDS

To make the dressing, put the sugar and vinegar in a saucepan and place on a low heat. Add a drop of water and stir to dissolve the sugar. Allow to cool, then place in a large jar with the oil and soy sauce and shake to combine.

Place the cabbage in a serving bowl and add the almonds and sesame seeds. Pour over the dressing and toss to combine.

Serves 4, generously

Talia was always a great fan of chef, Neil Perry. Many years ago, she ate a version of this veal dish in his restuarant, and then made her own delicious adaptation of it the very next Friday. It has become one of the family's most loved and often requested dishes, and now serves as such a fond reminder of her.

If you do not keep kosher, you can substitute butter for the margarine, and once you turn the cutlets over after frying the first side, sprinkle each with a tablespoon of freshly grated parmesan, before making the sauce.

VEAL CUTLETS WITH LEMON AND CAPERS

8 VEAL CUTLETS FROM THE RACK, SEPARATED, TRIMMED AND FLATTENED UNTIL 5 MM THICK
2 EGGS, BEATEN IN A WIDE BOWL
200 G (2 CUPS) DRY BREADCRUMBS, SEASONED GENEROUSLY WITH SALT AND PEPPER
125 ML (½ CUP) OLIVE OIL
125 G MARGARINE
JUICE OF 2 LEMONS
80 G (6 TABLESPOONS) BABY CAPERS, RINSED AND DRAINED

Put the cutlets into the bowl with the beaten egg for 15 minutes. Remove and immediately roll the cutlets in the breadcrumbs.

In a hot frying pan, heat 60 ml (¼ cup) of the olive oil and 40 g of the margarine. When the margarine has melted, add the veal cutlets, four at a time, and fry on a medium heat until golden. You will know to turn them over when the pink juice comes to the surface. Cook the other side until golden brown and just pink in the centre. Remove and drain on paper towel. Add the remaining oil and another 40 g of margarine to the pan, and repeat with the remaining cutlets. Remove and drain on paper towel, but leave the frying pan on the heat.

Into the hot pan, which should still have some oil in it, add the lemon juice and capers. Boil and stir for a minute or so, scraping up all the sediment from the base of the pan, until the juice reduces a little. Add the remaining margarine and stir for 1 minute until the sauce is bubbling and combined.

Return all the cutlets to the pan. Spoon some sauce over the cutlets and heat through. Serve with wilted spinach and couscous or soft polenta, with extra sauce poured over the top.

Serves 4–6

Talia became an excellent pastry and tart cook, inspired by the French Michelin-starred chefs, whose restaurants she frequented and whose food she often tried to re-create at home.

Locally, she was inspired by Damien Pignolet, and his legendary tarts. This raspberry tart also became legendary in Talia's family. The pastry recipe comes from Damien himself (with the added short cut of using the food processor) and she always said this was the best, easiest and most delicious one to make.

TALIA'S RASPBERRY TART

PASTRY
180 G COLD UNSALTED BUTTER,
    CHOPPED
240 G PLAIN FLOUR
60 ML (¼ CUP) ICE-COLD WATER
PINCH OF SALT

FILLING
200 ML DOUBLE OR THICKENED
    CREAM
2 EGGS
4 EGG YOLKS
140 G (⅔ CUP) CASTER SUGAR
300 G RASPBERRIES (FRESH
    OR FROZEN)

You will need a 26–28 cm tart tin with a removable base.

To make the pastry, put the butter, flour, water and salt in a food processor and pulse until just combined. Process quickly until a ball is formed. Place on a work surface and pat gently into a smooth ball, then flatten into a disc. Cover with plastic wrap and refrigerate for 30 minutes.

Roll out the pastry between two pieces of baking paper until 3 mm thick. Remove the top piece of paper, gently turn the pastry over and lay it over the tart tin. Remove the top piece of paper and gently press the pastry into the tin. Cover with foil (pressing the foil into the corners and over the side of the tin) and place in the freezer for 20 minutes. Meanwhile, preheat the oven to 180°C.

Fill the foil-lined tart with pastry weights or dried beans and blind bake for 15–20 minutes until no longer raw. Remove the weights and foil carefully and bake for a further 15 minutes or so, until the pastry is golden and cooked through.

Increase the oven to 190°C. To make the filling, place the cream, eggs, egg yolks and sugar in a bowl and whisk well, making sure the sugar dissolves. Arrange the raspberries in the bottom of the cooked tart shell (points up) in concentric circles. Carefully pour the filling over the top. Bake for 40 minutes, or until set. Serve at room temperature with cream.

Serves 10

Lena Goldstein

My family originated in Poland, starting out in Brest-Litovsk, then Lublin (where I was born) and then Warsaw. They had moved to Warsaw in search of a more secure life, but unfortunately this was not to be. Through some luck I survived the war, spending it mostly in the Warsaw Ghetto. With the help of another family, I managed to escape the ghetto and spent the last few years of the war in hiding, in a claustrophobic underground bunker. After the war, I thought I was the only one of my family remaining. While I was working as a correspondent for the Jewish Committee, which helped reunite survivors with their families, I heard news that my sister and her husband (who had been exiled to Siberia) were still alive. We were ecstatically reunited.

I married in Poland, and Olec and I came out to Australia in 1949 on the Italian ship, the Continental. After sixty years of marriage, Olec passed away in 2007. We have two sons and six grandsons. Although I'm in my nineties, I still enjoy baking and am so happy to be sharing my recipes with future generations.

Bienenstich — honey almond squares — means 'bee's sting' in German. This Viennese recipe was given to me by a German friend, who had immigrated to Sydney before the war. It's now a favourite of my son Martin and his son Daniel, both of whom have learnt to make it. I often make this when my friends come over to play cards. They don't come purely for my cake and tea — it's the card game they really come for!

BIENENSTICH

BASE

125 G UNSALTED BUTTER,
   AT ROOM TEMPERATURE
2 EGG YOLKS
100 G (⅔ CUP) PLAIN FLOUR
100 G (⅔ CUP) SELF-RAISING
   FLOUR
60 G (¼ CUP) SUGAR
2 TEASPOONS VANILLA EXTRACT

TOPPING

125 G UNSALTED BUTTER
100 G SUGAR
2 TABLESPOONS HONEY
155 G (1 CUP) CHOPPED ALMONDS

Preheat the oven to 180°C. Grease or line a 32 x 27 x 2 cm baking tin.

To make the base, combine the ingredients in a bowl and mix with your hands, squeezing the pastry together. Press the mixture into the base of the prepared tin and set aside.

To make the topping, melt the butter, sugar and honey in a saucepan, then add the almonds and stir to combine. Pour over the pastry base and spread out. Bake for 40–45 minutes until golden. Allow to cool in the tin, then remove and cut into squares. Store in an airtight container.

Makes 24 squares

Kindlech are a type of strudel biscuit filled with nuts, jam, chocolate and sultanas. I devised the filling, but the recipe for this thin flaky pastry was given to me by an elderly Polish lady many years ago. The pastry also makes wonderful hamantashen and cheese pockets.

KINDLECH

PASTRY

2 EGG YOLKS

250 G UNSALTED BUTTER, AT ROOM
  TEMPERATURE, CHOPPED

1 TABLESPOON SUGAR

2 TEASPOONS VANILLA EXTRACT

150 G SOUR CREAM

480 G PLAIN FLOUR

FILLING, PER ROLL

1 HEAPED TABLESPOON
  CHOCOLATE-HAZELNUT SPREAD

1 HEAPED TABLESPOON
  STRAWBERRY OR RASPBERRY JAM

1 HANDFUL OF LIGHTLY CRUSHED
  WALNUTS

1 SMALL HANDFUL OF SULTANAS

1 EGG YOLK, BEATEN, FOR
  GLAZING

Start this recipe the day before. To make the pastry, mix all the ingredients together with your hands (or quickly in the food processor) to make a soft but slightly sticky dough. Divide in two, wrap in plastic wrap and refrigerate overnight.

Preheat the oven to 180°C. Grease or line a large baking tray.

Cut each piece of dough into four equal pieces (each piece will make one roll). Working with one piece at a time, knead the dough on a board sprinkled with a little flour. Roll out thinly until you have a rough rectangle measuring about 30 x 15 cm. The pastry should be a little translucent.

Spread the chocolate-hazelnut and jam over the pastry, to the edges, and sprinkle with the walnuts and sultanas. Roll up from the long side to form a log and then place seam side down on the prepared tray. Brush with the egg yolk and prick a few times with a fork to let the air escape and prevent cracking. Bake for 45 minutes, or until golden. When cool, use a sharp serrated knife to cut each piece on the diagonal into ten slices.

Makes 8 rolls (or a total of 80 pieces)

Merrylin Goodman

My life with food was preordained. Mum, in the early stages of labour, yearning to bake a cake, whipped up eight cakes a few hours before I was born! Combining her love of food and entertaining, it came as no surprise that she decided to enter the restaurant business. So from a young age I was surrounded by chefs, waitresses — and food.

My parents were both born in London and came to Australia as teenagers, but their cooking was influenced by their Russian, Polish and Lithuanian backgrounds — from hot salt beef and chopped liver, latkes and wonderful gefilte fish, to many wondrous desserts and cakes. I guess it was beschert that I would love food, too. I became a home economist and then a cooking teacher for many years. I also ran my own kosher cookery school. My children appreciate and love preparing delicious food, and hopefully one day they will pass on that passion and knowledge to their children. And the door's always open for them to come home and enjoy my cooking!

This is a clear family favourite of ours. Cooking the beef slowly renders it fabulously soft and succulent. It is traditionally served hot with mashed potato, mustard and pickled cucumbers, or as a sandwich filling on rye bread.

SALT BEEF

1–1.5 KG PIECE PICKLED (CORNED)
    BEEF BRISKET OR BOLAR (BLADE)
1 ONION, QUARTERED
2 CLOVES GARLIC
2–3 BAY LEAVES
1 TEASPOON MUSTARD SEEDS
1 TEASPOON PEPPERCORNS
2 TABLESPOONS CIDER OR MALT
    VINEGAR
1 TABLESPOON BROWN SUGAR
SPRINKLE OF CHILLI FLAKES

Rinse the beef and put it in a stockpot or large saucepan. Cover with water and add the remaining ingredients. Slowly bring to the boil, then simmer gently for 1–1½ hours, or until the beef is tender when pierced with a fork. Remove the pot from the heat, but leave the beef in the water until ready to use. Slice and serve hot or cold.

Serves 4–6

Sharon Green

My father was stationed in India with the RAF during the war. When he returned to England, he decided he wanted to start afresh in a warmer, sunnier country. He and my mother married in September 1948, and they set sail to Australia a month later.

My mother was an exceptional baker and skilled cake decorator, and there was always a steady stream of family and friends popping in for a cup of tea and the sweet delicacies that she loved to bake. My husband, Stephen, comes from an entirely different ethnic and culinary background. It was his mother, Rhoda, who introduced me to an American-European style of cooking that I hadn't come across before. But it is from my mother that I inherited my sweet tooth. She taught me how to cook and bake, and showed me the untold pleasure in giving — and for that I am eternally grateful.

This is my version of a recipe from American Gourmet magazine. Adding a piece of this brittle to a simple poached peach or scoop of ice cream will turn an ordinary dessert into something special.

PUMPKIN SEED BRITTLE

220 G (1 CUP) SUGAR
125 ML (½ CUP) WATER
½ TEASPOON SALT
120 G (¾ CUP) RAW GREEN
  PUMPKIN SEEDS

Place a large sheet of baking paper (about 60 x 30 cm) on a work surface or on a board. Put the sugar, water and salt in a heavy-based saucepan on a medium heat and bring to the boil, stirring until the sugar is dissolved. Cook, without stirring, until the syrup reaches 116°C (240°F) (soft-ball stage) on a sugar thermometer (this will take 10–12 minutes). Remove the pan from the heat and stir in the pumpkin seeds with a wooden spoon. Stir for 4–5 minutes, or until the syrup crystallises.

Return the saucepan to a medium heat and cook, stirring constantly, for 10–12 minutes until the sugar melts completely (the sugar will continue to dry and become grainy before melting) and turns a deep caramel colour. Carefully pour the hot mixture onto the baking paper and then cover with another sheet of paper. Working quickly, use a rolling pin to firmly roll out the brittle as thinly as possible. Remove the top sheet of paper and cut the brittle into pieces with a heavy knife. Cool completely, then peel off the bottom piece of paper. Alternatively, break the brittle into pieces once cool. Store in an airtight container for 2 weeks, with the layers separated by pieces of baking paper.

Makes a 60 x 30 cm slab

I picked up the idea for this recipe from a newspaper in Israel several years ago. I am always looking for fat-free recipes and this fitted the bill. These biscotti are a standby in our house as they keep well and are a great pick-me-up, and different fruit and nuts can be substituted according to taste. Being kosher, it's good to have something sweet on hand that can be served with a meat or milk meal.

FRUIT AND NUT BISCOTTI

500 G (3⅓ CUPS) PLAIN FLOUR
500 G (2¼ CUPS) SUGAR
1 TABLESPOON BAKING POWDER
5 EGGS, LIGHTLY BEATEN
100 G (⅔ CUP) SULTANAS
100 G (½ CUP FIRMLY PACKED)
   DRIED APRICOTS, SLICED
100 G (½ CUP) PITTED DATES,
   CHOPPED
100 G (¾ CUP) PISTACHIO OR
   BRAZIL NUTS
100 G (⅔ CUP) WHOLE BLANCHED
   ALMONDS
100 G (¾ CUP) HAZELNUTS
FINELY GRATED ZEST OF 2 LEMONS

Preheat the oven to 180°C. Line two baking trays.

Combine the flour, sugar and baking powder in a large bowl. Add the beaten egg, a little at a time, until the dough takes shape but isn't too wet. You may not need to use all the egg. Add the fruit, nuts and lemon zest and mix well.

Divide the dough into six pieces. Wet your hands and form the dough into sausages, about 3 cm in diameter. Place the dough pieces well apart on the prepared trays and flatten slightly. Bake for 20–30 minutes, or until the biscotti are golden. Remove from the oven and leave for 10 minutes to cool and firm up.

Reduce the oven to 140°C. With a serrated knife, cut the biscotti on an angle into 5 mm thick slices and lay on the baking trays. Return to the oven and bake for 12 minutes, then turn them over and bake for a further 10–15 minutes, or until the biscotti are a pale golden colour (the baking time will vary depending on the thickness). Remove from the oven and cool on a wire rack. Store in an airtight container for up to 10 days.

Makes about 100 biscotti

Viv Green

I treasure my late mother's lovely handwritten recipes. Although she did not talk about her early life in Vienna, I was able to get a taste of her birthplace through the food she cooked. My parents fled Austria during the war as newlyweds. Taking very little with them, they managed to get to London, and from there they sailed to Australia.

Mummy was a great cook, and I would enjoy nothing better than sitting on a stool, watching her, just as she probably did with her mother. I loved those times. Over the years I enticed her to write down her recipes or just make notes, and I am so pleased I did. Some years later my son was born, and he too grew to love cooking. At the age of three he would stand on a stool and help me — stirring rice, mixing batter, licking the beaters — as we cooked from my mother's basic recipes. Now he has his own family and encourages his children to get their hands dirty in the kitchen. He loves to entertain and I'm sure whenever he cooks, somewhere in the back of his mind, he remembers his Oma.

Kaffee und kuchen *is a Viennese custom and you can't have one without the other. As Mum would say, 'All you need is a good coffee and a piece of cake.' Her apricot cake is one of my favourites. It's simple, delicious and she made it often, sometimes substituting plums or cherries for the apricots. Whenever I make this I think of her and all the good times we shared.*

APRICOT CAKE

4 EGGS, SEPARATED

330 G (1½ CUPS) SUGAR

250 G UNSALTED BUTTER, AT ROOM TEMPERATURE

300 G (2 CUPS) SELF-RAISING FLOUR

800 G TIN APRICOT HALVES, DRAINED

Preheat the oven to 180°C. Grease or line a lamington tin or baking tin (about 32 x 27 x 3 cm).

Beat the egg whites until stiff peaks form. In a separate bowl, beat the egg yolks and sugar until light and fluffy. Add the butter to the yolk mixture and beat until creamy, then mix in the flour. Fold in a spoonful of the egg whites by hand to lighten the batter, then continue to fold in the remaining egg whites until just incorporated.

Spoon the mixture into the prepared tin and place the apricots on top, cut side up. Bake for 45 minutes, or until a skewer inserted into the cake comes out clean. Dust with icing sugar before serving if desired.

Serves 16

Eva Grunstein

When Eva looked back over her life, and the turmoil of the years lived through the war, she would then look at her lovely family, and remember how blessed she was and how many wonderful miracles took place along the way.

Eva was born in Romania and moved to Australia in 1949, after the Holocaust. Her mother had an antique shop and often travelled on business so, at fifteen, Eva took over the running of the kitchen. She often recalled her father's words of praise: 'You know, you cook better than your mother.'

Eva came to Australia as a single mother. Her first job was as a dishwasher at Chateaux Pierre in Leura. One day the cook was sick, and suddenly she was making dobos torte for the patrons — and they loved it! Slowly life got better and better. She married and had another beautiful child. She worked in a hotel at Bondi Beach and also earned a bit of extra money stitching stockings, a skill she learned from the old country. After Eva was widowed, she married Jim Grunstein. Sadly Eva has now passed away, but she will always be remembered for her generosity of spirit, and how much she loved to cook for all her family.

This is one of the most light and moist chiffon cakes imaginable, with a lovely orange flavour.
Once mastered, you will make it over and over.

ORANGE CHIFFON CAKE

8 EGGS, SEPARATED
345 G (1½ CUPS) CASTER SUGAR
185 ML (¾ CUP) VEGETABLE OIL
185 ML (¾ CUP) FRESH ORANGE
   JUICE (ABOUT 3 ORANGES)
FINELY GRATED ZEST OF ½ LEMON
225 G (1½ CUPS) SELF-RAISING
   FLOUR, SIFTED

Preheat the oven to 180°C. You will need an angel cake (chiffon) tin (see note, page 35). Do not grease it.

Whisk the egg whites until soft peaks form. Slowly add 115 g (½ cup) of the sugar and continue whisking until the egg whites are stiff but not dry. In a separate bowl, beat the egg yolks and the remaining sugar until light and fluffy. Add the oil and keep beating for a couple of minutes until well combined.

Add the orange juice and lemon zest. Add the flour carefully, then beat to make sure the flour is well combined. Gently fold the egg whites into the flour mixture with a metal spoon, until just mixed through. Pour the mixture into the cake tin and bake for 1 hour, or until a skewer inserted into the cake comes out clean.

After removing the cake from the oven, immediately invert it to cool by balancing the middle funnel onto a bottle neck. (The cake will be dangling upside down.) It is important for the cake to be inverted and suspended upside down until it is cool to stop it from collapsing. When cool, run a knife around the outside of the cake and the funnel. Lift the base out of the tin, then use the knife to ease the cake off the base.

Serves 12

WIZO was Eva's passion, and over the years she made so many wonderful friends through their meetings. She was always happy to bake and serve this cake, and everyone loved eating it — maybe that's why so many women turned up! This cheesecake is best served the day it is made, but if you have any left over, put it in the microwave for a few seconds to refresh.

HUNGARIAN CHEESECAKE

DOUGH
300 G (2 CUPS) SELF-RAISING
   FLOUR, PLUS EXTRA FOR
   SPRINKLING
125 G UNSALTED BUTTER, AT ROOM
   TEMPERATURE
2 EGGS
110 G (½ CUP) SUGAR
60 ML (¼ CUP) MILK
DASH OF VANILLA EXTRACT

FILLING
8 EGGS, SEPARATED
750 G FARM CHEESE
300 ML THICKENED CREAM
230 G (1 CUP) CASTER SUGAR
1 TEASPOON VANILLA EXTRACT
2 TABLESPOONS SELF-RAISING
   FLOUR

Preheat the oven to 180°C. Grease and flour a 33 x 23 cm cake tin or baking dish.

The dough is best mixed using an electric mixer, as it is too soft to touch. Put the flour in the bowl, add the butter and beat until it resembles coarse breadcrumbs. Add the eggs, sugar, milk and vanilla and mix well until a dough is formed. Divide the dough in half. Using half the dough, place spoonfuls into the prepared cake tin, to form the base. Sprinkle extra flour on top of each spoonful and gently pat the dough into place.

To make the filling, combine all the ingredients, except the egg whites, and beat until well combined. In a separate bowl, whisk the egg whites with a pinch of salt until stiff. Fold the egg whites into the cheese mixture, then pour this on top of the dough base.

Flour the work surface and roll the remaining dough into long thin sausages. Flatten these slightly to form strips, and place on top of the cheesecake to form a lattice design. Bake for 1 hour until golden.

Serves 16

This slice, pronounced 'jerbo', was originally made by the famous Gerbeaud Cafe in Budapest, which Eva visited. Zserbo slice became an essential part of the coffee and cake culture, created by the unique Hungarian Sydney Jewish community. It is a special treat, which keeps incredibly well in the fridge and always impresses people when they drop over.

ZSERBO SLICE

PASTRY

1 x 7 G SACHET DRIED YEAST

125 ML (½ CUP) WARM MILK

1 TABLESPOON SUGAR

420 G (2¾ CUPS) PLAIN FLOUR

250 G UNSALTED BUTTER, CHOPPED

4 EGG YOLKS

2 HEAPED TABLESPOONS SOUR CREAM

WALNUT FILLING

500 G (4⅓ CUPS) FINELY GROUND WALNUTS

1 TABLESPOON VEGETABLE OIL

60 ML (¼ CUP) SWEET SACRAMENTAL WINE OR PORT

230 G (1 CUP) CASTER SUGAR

4 TABLESPOONS APRICOT JAM

CHOCOLATE GANACHE

150 ML PURE CREAM (35% FAT)

125 G DARK CHOCOLATE, CHOPPED

1 TABLESPOON LEMON JUICE

Preheat the oven to 180°C. Grease and line (with an overhang) a 33 x 23 cm cake tin or baking dish.

To make the pastry, mix the yeast, warm milk and sugar in a small bowl. Leave for a few minutes until the mixture starts to froth. In a larger bowl, mix together the flour and butter with your fingertips until it resembles breadcrumbs. Add the egg yolks, sour cream and yeast mixture and mix well. Knead for a few minutes on a floured surface until smooth. Set aside.

To make the walnut filling, combine the ground walnuts, oil, wine and sugar. Add more wine or sugar to taste. Set aside.

Divide the pastry into three pieces. Roll out one piece to fit the base of the cake tin and lay the pastry on the base. If needed, cut and patch the pastry to ensure the base is covered. Spread half the apricot jam and then half the walnut mixture over the pastry. Pat down gently. Roll out a second piece of pastry and repeat the layers. Roll out the last piece of pastry and place on the top. Bake for 30 minutes, or until golden. Remove from the oven and allow to cool in the tin.

Meanwhile, to make the chocolate ganache, heat the cream to almost boiling point, then remove the pan from the heat and add the chocolate. Stir until smooth. Stir in the lemon juice (the lemon juice will give a nice shine when set). Allow to cool a little, until the liquid is of a pouring consistency. Pour the ganache over the top of the slice, then spread to cover. Leave to set in the fridge, then cut into small rectangles. The slice is best served at room temperature.

Makes 24 slices

Karen Gutman

The kitchen in my maternal grandmother's house was the true heart of her home. Perhaps Mama Elke's Polish upbringing determined that her whole week was spent preparing for Friday night. Each week she liked to eat at one daughter's house, but she would then deliver a complete dinner to her other two daughters and their families. That meant gefilte fish, chicken soup with kneidlach or lokshen, chopped liver, apple compote and, of course, a cake. My father, however, comes from a very different life, being sixth-generation Australian.

Partly due to Mama Elke's influence and definitely because I find cooking so relaxing and enjoyable (and I love to eat!), I spend a lot of time in the kitchen, cooking almost anything and everything. I believe that if you can read you can cook, so I am never frightened to try a new recipe. Our kitchen is also the heart of our household. My husband, Michael, encourages me to try new dishes, and our three kids have always loved being in the kitchen with me. In our home, it's absolutely where all the action is.

When we moved to London, we found ourselves experiencing real winters for the first time. With half my family being vegetarian, I searched for nourishing recipes that were also delicious and warming. This soup is inspired by a recipe from food writer Marlena Spieler. It is best made with good-quality rich stock rather than cubes, and close to serving time. It also makes a great side dish if left to stand and thicken.

Israeli couscous soup

1 TABLESPOON OLIVE OIL
1 LARGE ONION, FINELY CHOPPED
1 HEAPED TEASPOON GROUND CUMIN
2 x 400 G TINS DICED TOMATOES
1.5 LITRES (6 CUPS) CHICKEN OR VEGETABLE STOCK
250 G ISRAELI COUSCOUS
1 BUNCH PARSLEY, CHOPPED

Heat the olive oil in a large saucepan, add the onion and fry for 10 minutes, or until light brown in colour. Add the cumin and stir through the onion for a few minutes. Add the tomatoes and stock, season generously with salt and pepper to taste, and simmer gently for 20 minutes, uncovered.

Add the couscous and cook for a further 8–12 minutes, or until the couscous is cooked through. Taste to check the seasoning. You may need to add up to a cup of extra stock if the soup is too thick or has been left to stand before serving. Stir the parsley through to serve.

Serves 6

This cake came to me from an old Melbourne friend Gina Swart, who has made it for many years at Rosh Hashanah. It is, without a doubt, the best, most moist and delicious honey cake around. Its name came from the time when Gina was avidly pouring the mixtures into the mixing bowl and got too close — her hair got caught around the whisking beaters, which pulled half of it out! We all laugh every time we make the cake, and every time we share the recipe with friends we tell the story and laugh again.

GINA'S HAIR-RAISING HONEY CAKE

25 G (¼ CUP) DRY BREADCRUMBS
375 ML (1½ CUPS) HOT TAP WATER

DRY MIXTURE
225 G (1½ CUPS) PLAIN FLOUR
225 G (1½ CUPS) SELF-RAISING
  FLOUR
1½ TEASPOONS BICARBONATE
  OF SODA
40 G (⅓ CUP) COCOA POWDER

WET MIXTURE
4 EGGS
345 G (1½ CUPS) CASTER SUGAR
185 ML (¾ CUP) VEGETABLE OIL
500 G HONEY
DASH OF VANILLA EXTRACT

Preheat the oven to 180°C. Grease a large 26 cm x 10 cm deep angel cake tin. It is best to use a tin without a removable base, as the mixture is liquid and may leak. Sprinkle the base and side of the tin with breadcrumbs, tipping out any excess.

For the dry mixture, sift the dry ingredients together into a bowl. For the wet mixture, in a separate large bowl (or electric mixer bowl), mix the wet ingredients together until well combined. Mix the dry mixture into the wet mixture, alternating with the hot water.

Pour into the prepared cake tin. Bake for 1 hour, or until a skewer inserted in the cake comes out clean. Allow the cake to cool before turning out of the tin.

Serves 12

Ken Hacker

What better inspiration for my own cooking than my parents? My mother was quite the Sachertorte expert. When her mother visited she made it using twelve eggs, as was the Czech way, but when her mother-in-law visited she used twenty, as was the Viennese tradition. What a peacemaker! My father also loved cooking. Every week he liked to cook something sweet; in fact, each item he prepared was sweeter than the week before. Imagine — he cooked until he was 91!

I was born in Austria in 1923, leaving my homeland in 1938 because of the terrible situation in Vienna. We sailed first to London to 'learn the language' and then to Sydney. Some years later I married my lovely wife, Aviva. Together with our four children we embraced life in Sydney. I've had many interesting and varied careers: a scientific glass blower, boilermaker, an actor, artist, magician, and I played the electric guitar in the band, Kenny Hacker and the Royal Hawaiians. I have been involved all my life with charities serving the local, worldwide and Jewish communities.

Sunday night is my turn to cook, when Aviva allows me in the kitchen. I love to make one of the old favourites: Salzburger nockerl (a sweet soufflé), macaroni cheese, plum dumplings (zwetschkenknoedel), spaetzle or goulash. Our children and grandchildren adore these old-world dishes, and seeing them so happy gives me great joy in return.

When I was about thirteen and living in Vienna, my parents sent me off to Scout Camp for a few months. I wanted desperately to earn my cook's badge and, to do so, I pledged to cook 300 plum dumplings for sixty ravenous boys. I started at 3 a.m., with a deadline of noon. It was much harder than I anticipated and they weren't ready until 3 p.m. — and all my hard work was devoured in an astonishing 4 minutes. Because I was so late, I never did receive that badge, although the dumplings have now become a family recipe and something our children always associate with me.

Apricot or plum dumplings

1 KG POTATOES (PREFERABLY
   KIPFLER OR NICOLA), UNPEELED,
   WASHED
300 G (2 CUPS) PLAIN FLOUR
1 EGG
½ TEASPOON SALT
20 VERY SMALL APRICOTS OR
   PLUMS (PREFERABLY ANGELINA),
   WASHED AND DRIED WELL
10 SUGAR CUBES, HALVED
100 G (1 CUP) DRY BREADCRUMBS
125 G UNSALTED BUTTER
CASTER SUGAR, FOR SPRINKLING

Start this recipe the day before. Boil the potatoes until very soft. Drain and when just cool enough to handle, peel and mash. Add the flour, egg and salt and mix through to make a dough, kneading for a couple of minutes only. Cover with plastic wrap and leave the dough to rest overnight in the fridge. When ready to use, knead lightly with a little flour until you have a nice, soft malleable dough.

Prepare the apricots or plums by cutting them in half. Remove the stones and replace with a halved sugar cube. Close the fruit. If you prefer, you can omit the sugar and leave the fruit whole.

Roll out a small piece of dough (about 75 g) on a well-floured board to make a 9–10 cm diameter circle, 3–4 mm thick. Place the fruit in the middle and bring the dough up to fully enclose the fruit. With floury hands, shape into a smooth ball, ensuring that it is fully sealed. Set aside on a floured plate until ready to use. Repeat with the remaining dough and fruit.

In a small frying pan, toast three-quarters of the breadcrumbs until brown. Remove the pan from the heat and add the butter, stirring to combine. Add the remaining breadcrumbs and mix through. Set aside.

Bring a large pot of water to the boil. Working in batches, carefully place the dumplings in the water (the number you cook depends on the size of your pot; be careful not to overcrowd). Simmer for 15–20 minutes, or until the dough is cooked through. Remove from the pot with a slotted spoon and roll in the buttery breadcrumbs. Sprinkle each dumpling with caster sugar and serve immediately.

Makes about 20

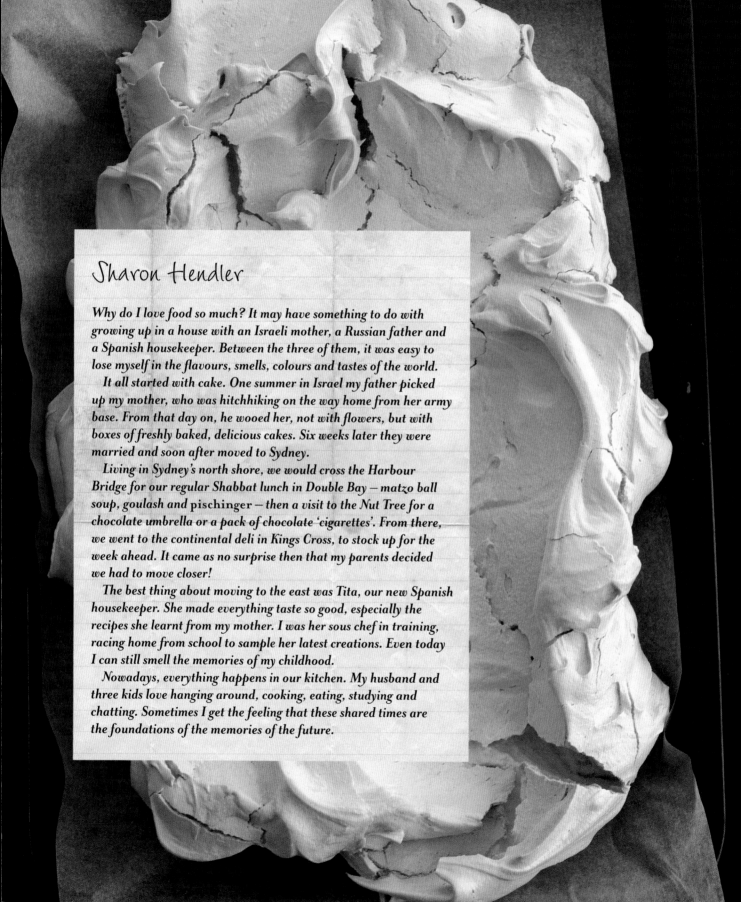

Sharon Hendler

Why do I love food so much? It may have something to do with growing up in a house with an Israeli mother, a Russian father and a Spanish housekeeper. Between the three of them, it was easy to lose myself in the flavours, smells, colours and tastes of the world.

It all started with cake. One summer in Israel my father picked up my mother, who was hitchhiking on the way home from her army base. From that day on, he wooed her, not with flowers, but with boxes of freshly baked, delicious cakes. Six weeks later they were married and soon after moved to Sydney.

Living in Sydney's north shore, we would cross the Harbour Bridge for our regular Shabbat lunch in Double Bay — matzo ball soup, goulash and pischinger — then a visit to the Nut Tree for a chocolate umbrella or a pack of chocolate 'cigarettes'. From there, we went to the continental deli in Kings Cross, to stock up for the week ahead. It came as no surprise then that my parents decided we had to move closer!

The best thing about moving to the east was Tita, our new Spanish housekeeper. She made everything taste so good, especially the recipes she learnt from my mother. I was her sous chef in training, racing home from school to sample her latest creations. Even today I can still smell the memories of my childhood.

Nowadays, everything happens in our kitchen. My husband and three kids love hanging around, cooking, eating, studying and chatting. Sometimes I get the feeling that these shared times are the foundations of the memories of the future.

This recipe is adapted from a cooking course I did in Tuscany a few years ago with the wonderful Joanne Weir. It's what I like best about winter.

TUSCAN BEAN SOUP

400 G TIN CANNELLINI BEANS,
   RINSED AND DRAINED
1 TABLESPOON EXTRA-VIRGIN
   OLIVE OIL
½ STALK CELERY, FINELY DICED
3 CARROTS, PEELED AND DICED
1 WHOLE HEAD CAVOLO NERO
   (OR ¼ SAVOY CABBAGE), DICED
1 LEEK, WHITE AND PALE GREEN
   PART ONLY, DICED
3 POTATOES, PEELED AND DICED
1 ONION, DICED
1 TABLESPOON TOMATO PASTE
1 LITRE (4 CUPS) CHICKEN OR
   VEGETABLE STOCK
1 LITRE (4 CUPS) WATER
EXTRA-VIRGIN OLIVE OIL,
   FOR DRIZZLING
FINELY GRATED PARMESAN CHEESE
   (OPTIONAL), TO SERVE

Place half the cannellini beans in a blender or food processor and process until smooth, adding a little water if necessary.

Heat the olive oil in a soup pot or large saucepan on a medium heat. Add the celery, carrots, cabbage, leek, potatoes, onion and tomato paste. Pour in the stock and enough of the water to cover the vegetables by 2 cm. Simmer for about 2 hours, or until the vegetables are very soft. Add the beans (whole and puréed) and simmer for a further 5 minutes. Season to taste with salt and freshly ground black pepper.

Let the soup cool for at least 1 hour, or preferably overnight. To serve, bring to the boil. Serve drizzled with the olive oil and sprinkled with parmesan cheese if desired.

Serves 6–8

Before I got married, I was given Margaret Fulton's Encyclopedia of Food and Cookery, *which I still use today. This pavlova recipe comes from that book and I have been making it for over twenty years. I always double the recipe and both cook and serve it on a huge ceramic serving platter.*

PAVLOVA

6 EGG WHITES, AT ROOM
   TEMPERATURE
PINCH OF SALT
460 G (2 CUPS) CASTER SUGAR
1½ TEASPOONS VANILLA EXTRACT
1½ TEASPOONS VINEGAR

TOPPING
300 ML PURE CREAM (35% FAT)
ICING SUGAR, TO TASTE
500 G (2 PUNNETS) STRAWBERRIES,
   HULLED AND SLICED
6 PASSIONFRUIT
3 BANANAS, SLICED

Preheat the oven to 150°C. Grease an ovenproof platter, about dinner-plate size.

To make the meringue base, whisk the egg whites with the salt until soft peaks form, then add the sugar, a tablespoon at a time, mixing continuously until all the sugar is incorporated. Whisk until glossy, then using a metal spoon, gently fold in the vanilla and vinegar.

Pile the meringue on top of the platter and flatten a little with a spatula. Bake for 45 minutes, then turn the oven off and leave the pavlova in the oven for 1 hour, with the door closed.

For the topping, whip the cream with about 1 tablespoon icing sugar, or to taste, until it is stiff. When the meringue has cooled completely, top with the whipped cream and the fruit. You can make this ahead of time and refrigerate the meringue with the cream until needed, and add the fruit just before serving.

Serves 8–10

I first tasted these delicious rusk-like biscuits in the early playgroup days with my son Ariel, who is now seventeen. One of the other mothers, Vikki Biggs, always had them at her house and they were brilliant. She finally admitted that the recipe came from her grandmother, Nanny Rahil, who eventually came and showed us how to make them.

SOUHARIKI

2 EGGS, BEATEN WITH A FORK
   UNTIL FROTHY
230 G (1 CUP) CASTER SUGAR
185 ML (¾ CUP) VEGETABLE OIL
2 TEASPOONS VANILLA EXTRACT
1 HANDFUL OF SULTANAS
1 HANDFUL OF SLIVERED
   ALMONDS, TOASTED
225 G (1½ CUPS) PLAIN FLOUR
225 G (1½ CUPS) SELF-RAISING
   FLOUR

Preheat the oven to 180°C. Line a large baking tray.

Whisk together the eggs, sugar, oil, vanilla, sultanas and almonds. Add equal amounts of the flours until the dough mixes clean off the bowl. Divide the dough into four and roll each portion into a log, about 30 cm long. Place the log on the prepared tray and flatten slightly with your hands. Bake for 20 minutes, then reduce the oven to 170°C and bake for a further 5–10 minutes, or until slightly brown.

Remove from the oven and allow to rest for 5 minutes. Cut across into 2 cm thick slices, then place the slices flat on the baking tray. Reduce the oven to 110°C. Return the biscuits to the oven and cook for 1 hour, or until deep golden brown.

Makes about 50 biscuits

Gary Horwitz

A huge dining table dressed with crisp white tablecloths and green ivy wound around candelabras signalled Shabbat at my grandparents' (Pappy and Nettie) house in Saxonwold, South Africa. The bell rang for dinner, the kids raced in and grabbed their favourite seat in anticipation of an evening filled with laughter, stories, songs and traditional Lithuanian food.

I have all these wonderful memories, but I will never forget the day, many years ago, when my sister said to me, 'Nettie has died.' I asked her, 'What does that mean?' to which she sadly replied, 'No more Shabbat dinners.' That sparked in me a desire to create my own family Shabbat table one day, to give my children a taste of what I had experienced.

My love for food took me to Hotel School, and then I was fortunate to work in the kitchen of a two-star Michelin restaurant in London. There I learnt the basics of cooking and the workings of an English kitchen. I immigrated to Sydney in 1986 with my wife, Paula, and we opened The Swiss Deli in Double Bay. Nothing was bought in; we made everything in our kitchen. Turkey and mayonnaise, tongue and pickles, cheesecakes and blintzes, roast beef and brisket, chopped liver and biltong all marched out the door.

Today I love to cook whatever my friends and family like to eat. Cooking is my greatest passion; it relaxes me and provides a creative outlet. I make dinner for my family every night and secretly harbour a desire to be at the centre of an open-plan kitchen, cooking and entertaining the guests in a buzzing restaurant.

When we started The Swiss Deli, we had a large Jewish clientele and they wanted to buy many traditional Jewish foods. Chopped liver was one that everyone wanted, as no-one wanted to start at home with the livers and the mincing. We used to make an incredible 50 kilograms of this every week! You will need a mincer for this recipe.

CHOPPED LIVER

625 G CHICKEN LIVERS,
  THOROUGHLY WASHED AND
  CLEANED
4 LARGE ONIONS, SLICED
3 HEAPED TABLESPOONS SCHMALTZ
  (OR RENDERED CHICKEN FAT)
3 TABLESPOONS VEGETABLE OIL
3 HARD-BOILED EGGS
1½ TABLESPOONS SWEET
  SACRAMENTAL WINE OR PORT
2 HARD-BOILED EGGS, EXTRA,
  GRATED, FOR GARNISH

Put the chicken livers in a saucepan and cover with water, season with salt and pepper, and bring to the boil for about 5 minutes. Drain and rinse in cold water.

Fry the onions in the schmaltz and oil for about 20 minutes, or until soft, glassy and lightly browned. Mince the livers, onions, eggs, wine, salt and pepper together in a mincer. Do not use a food processor as it will be too smooth. Season to taste again with lots of salt and pepper. To serve, garnish with the grated egg.

Serves 8 as a starter

My father, Alec, also loves to cook. Years ago he went to France and did a cooking course, where he learnt how to make this soup. It has been part of our family repertoire ever since.

TOMATO SOUP WITH BASIL AND ROCKET OIL

1.5 LITRES (6 CUPS) GOOD-
   QUALITY VEGETABLE
   (OR CHICKEN) STOCK
60 ML (¼ CUP) EXTRA-VIRGIN
   OLIVE OIL
1 ONION, CHOPPED
3 CLOVES GARLIC, CRUSHED
1.5 KG VERY RIPE SOFT TOMATOES,
   CHOPPED
200 G STALE SOURDOUGH
   BREAD, CRUSTS REMOVED,
   THINLY SLICED OR MADE INTO
   BREADCRUMBS
200 G (2 CUPS) FRESHLY GRATED
   PARMESAN, PLUS EXTRA
   TO SERVE

BASIL AND ROCKET OIL
170 ML (⅔ CUP) EXTRA-VIRGIN
   OLIVE OIL
3 TABLESPOONS CHOPPED BASIL
3 TABLESPOONS CHOPPED ROCKET

To make the basil and rocket oil, put the olive oil, basil and rocket in a blender, season with sea salt and freshly ground black pepper and process until completely smooth.

Heat the stock in a large saucepan. Meanwhile, heat the olive oil in a large frying pan and fry the onion, garlic and tomatoes on a low heat for about 10 minutes until soft. Transfer to a food processor and blend, then stir the blended tomato mixture into the hot stock. Add the bread.

Cover and simmer gently for 45 minutes, or until thick and creamy. Give the soup a good whisk every now and then to break up the bread. Be careful, as this soup can catch on the bottom of the saucepan. Stir the parmesan into the soup and season with sea salt and freshly ground black pepper to taste. Serve hot, warm or cold, drizzled with the basil and rocket oil. Serve with extra parmesan and crusty bread.

Serves 8–10

I love inviting friends around to eat and drink on a Sunday afternoon. This is probably the most requested dish that I make. There is nothing better than a group of friends sitting round the table — beautifully set by the very talented Paula with candles and flowers — getting stuck into these little chickens, drinking wine and licking their fingers. If you do not keep kosher, substitute butter for the olive oil in the sauce.

BABY PERI PERI CHICKENS

12 X NO. 4 OR NO. 5 BABY
    CHICKENS, BUTTERFLIED

MARINADE
JUICE OF 3 LEMONS
1 TABLESPOON OLIVE OIL
60 ML (¼ CUP) WHITE VINEGAR
4 CLOVES GARLIC, CRUSHED
3 RED BIRD'S EYE CHILLIES,
    SEEDED AND FINELY CHOPPED
3 TABLESPOONS CHILLI FLAKES
3 TABLESPOONS SALT
1 TABLESPOON GROUND BLACK
    PEPPER

PERI PERI SAUCE
3 CLOVES GARLIC, CRUSHED
6 RED BIRD'S EYE CHILLIES,
    SEEDED AND FINELY CHOPPED
1 TEASPOON CHILLI POWDER
JUICE OF 2 LEMONS
1 TEASPOON WHITE VINEGAR
200 ML OLIVE OIL

To butterfly the chicken, place it breast side down (wings up) and split it with a knife down the backbone. Cut off and discard the neck. Place the 'open' side of the chicken down on the board and firmly press on the chicken, breaking the main joints so the bird is really flat (or ask the butcher to do this for you).

To make the marinade, mix together all the marinade ingredients. Rub the marinade into both sides of the chickens. Put the chickens into a large non-reactive dish, layering them in pairs, with the open side of one chicken facing the open side of the next. Cover and refrigerate for a minimum of 2 hours or overnight. Remove from the fridge 30 minutes before cooking.

Preheat the barbecue to its highest setting. Once hot, place the chickens skin side up on the barbecue and cook for 15 minutes, or until golden brown and almost cooked through. Turn the chickens over and cook them skin side down for 10–15 minutes, taking care that the skin doesn't burn. When the skin is well cooked, turn the barbecue down to low and turn the birds over again. Cover with a lid or foil and cook for a further 10 minutes, or until completely cooked through and the juice runs clear from the thigh when pierced.

To make the peri peri sauce, place the garlic, chillies, chilli powder, lemon juice and vinegar in a blender or food processor and process until well combined. Add the olive oil slowly through the feed tube until well amalgamated. This can also be done by hand with a whisk. Season generously to taste with salt and pepper, and add more chilli and lemon juice if needed. Pour the sauce over the hot chickens and serve. The peri peri sauce is also delicious made with 250 g of butter, melted, instead of olive oil, and goes well with grilled fish, too.

Serves 12, allowing one chicken per person

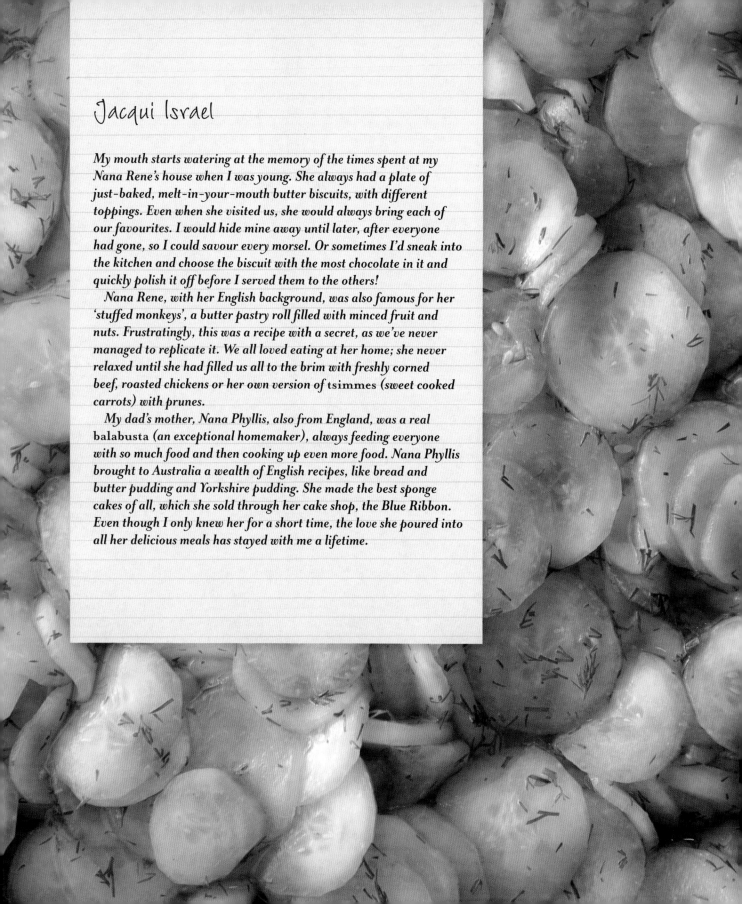

Jacqui Israel

My mouth starts watering at the memory of the times spent at my Nana Rene's house when I was young. She always had a plate of just-baked, melt-in-your-mouth butter biscuits, with different toppings. Even when she visited us, she would always bring each of our favourites. I would hide mine away until later, after everyone had gone, so I could savour every morsel. Or sometimes I'd sneak into the kitchen and choose the biscuit with the most chocolate in it and quickly polish it off before I served them to the others!

Nana Rene, with her English background, was also famous for her 'stuffed monkeys', a butter pastry roll filled with minced fruit and nuts. Frustratingly, this was a recipe with a secret, as we've never managed to replicate it. We all loved eating at her home; she never relaxed until she had filled us all to the brim with freshly corned beef, roasted chickens or her own version of tsimmes (sweet cooked carrots) with prunes.

My dad's mother, Nana Phyllis, also from England, was a real balabusta (an exceptional homemaker), always feeding everyone with so much food and then cooking up even more food. Nana Phyllis brought to Australia a wealth of English recipes, like bread and butter pudding and Yorkshire pudding. She made the best sponge cakes of all, which she sold through her cake shop, the Blue Ribbon. Even though I only knew her for a short time, the love she poured into all her delicious meals has stayed with me a lifetime.

I remember eating this salad at both my grandmothers' houses on Friday nights and at festival celebrations. Then it was made by my mother and now by me. It is easy, quick and refreshing and goes with so many things. It needs to be made several hours ahead of serving time.

CUCUMBER SALAD

3 TELEGRAPH CUCUMBERS,
    PEELED AND FINELY SLICED
SALT

DRESSING
125 ML (½ CUP) WHITE VINEGAR
60 ML (¼ CUP) WATER
2 TEASPOONS SUGAR
¼ BUNCH DILL, FINELY CHOPPED
    (OPTIONAL)

Place the cucumber slices in a colander, sprinkling with salt as you layer the slices on top of each other. Toss lightly, draining off any water. Leave for 3–4 hours in the colander, then drain again and place into a bowl.

To make the dressing, mix together the vinegar, water and sugar. Pour the dressing over the cucumbers and toss well to coat in the dressing. Add the dill and leave for another few hours or overnight before serving.

Serves 6 as a side dish

NANA PHYLLIS' BISCUITS

125 G BUTTER, AT ROOM
    TEMPERATURE, CHOPPED
250 G (1⅔ CUPS) SELF-RAISING
    FLOUR
90 G CASTER SUGAR
1 EGG
½ TEASPOON VANILLA EXTRACT
EXTRA FLOUR, FOR ROLLING
EXTRA CASTER SUGAR, FOR
    SPRINKLING

Preheat the oven to 180°C. Line two large baking trays.

Rub the butter into the flour with your fingertips until it resembles breadcrumbs. Add the sugar, then the egg and vanilla and combine well to make a soft dough.

Place the dough on a floured surface and roll out thinly (about 1–2 mm), flouring the rolling pin as necessary. Cut out the biscuits with a round cookie cutter or small glass. Place the biscuits on the prepared trays and sprinkle with the extra sugar. Bake for 10–12 minutes until just starting to brown. Cool a little on the trays, then transfer to a wire rack.

Makes 60 biscuits

NANA RENE'S BISCUITS

120 G SELF-RAISING FLOUR
120 G PLAIN FLOUR
120 G UNSALTED BUTTER,
    AT ROOM TEMPERATURE
120 G CASTER SUGAR
1 EGG, BEATEN
PINCH OF SALT
½ TEASPOON VANILLA EXTRACT
TOPPING OF CHOICE: DARK
    CHOCOLATE (SHAVED OR
    IN CHUNKS), BLANCHED
    OR SLIVERED ALMONDS,
    CINNAMON SUGAR, CHOPPED
    CRYSTALLISED GINGER

Preheat the oven to 175°C. Line two large baking trays.

Sift the flours together and set aside. Cream the butter and sugar, then add the egg, sifted flours, salt and vanilla. Combine to form a soft dough.

Roll the dough into 2 cm balls, place on the prepared trays and press very flat with your fingers. Use a floured fork to make imprints over the surface, all facing the same direction. Add the topping of your choice. Bake for 12 minutes, then remove from the oven and cool. Reduce the oven to 150°C, then return the biscuits to the oven and cook for a further 6–8 minutes until golden. Cool a little on the trays, then transfer to a wire rack.

Makes 45–50 biscuits

Hilary Jacobson

My mum was a great baker but, unusually for those times, she worked so was often short on time. I once asked her to bake me a cake that I needed for school and she suggested I try to make it myself. That day was to mark the beginning of my frequent and often messy career in the kitchen.

As my confidence grew, I experimented with a wide variety of ingredients and styles. I still cherish my first cookbook, the International Goodwill Recipe Book *(WIZO, South Africa) and have since bought a copy (now in its seventh edition) for each of my two children.*

I come from a large South African family and have very happy memories of huge family Sunday lunches with all my cousins, and the thrill of the Jewish holidays at my father's mother's house, Bobba. She was a great and abundant cook, just like her girth! My mother's father was a butcher and did most of the cooking for his family, which, according to Mum, was 'very fortunate' because her mother did not enjoy cooking. Luckily, he passed his love of food on to Mum, and she then passed it on to me.

When we moved to Australia in the 1980s, I was completely amazed and excited by the ingredients available here. I began to devote (and still do) my free time to cooking, and my husband, Ian, has been constantly subjected to my various experiments. He once respectfully asked if we could just eat some 'ordinary' food, like a stew or cottage pie!

Over many years of entertaining, I have become known for this dish. Served with crusty ciabatta and a simple green salad, these meatballs are unbeatable — and they're even better served the next day. If you do not keep kosher, add 200 g finely grated parmesan cheese to the meat mixture for an extra dimension and flavour. Another nice variation on this recipe is to brown the meatballs in olive oil before placing them in the sauce.

ITALIAN MEATBALLS

MEATBALLS

1 KG VEAL MINCE

2 ONIONS, VERY FINELY CHOPPED

2 EGGS, BEATEN

60 G STALE SOURDOUGH BREAD,
CRUST REMOVED, PROCESSED
TO MAKE ABOUT 1 CUP COARSE
BREADCRUMBS

125 ML (½ CUP) WATER

1 BUNCH FLAT-LEAF PARSLEY,
FINELY CHOPPED

SAUCE

20 VERY RIPE ROMA (PLUM)
TOMATOES, HALVED

10 CLOVES GARLIC, PEELED

125 ML (½ CUP) OLIVE OIL

3 ONIONS, COARSELY CHOPPED

375 ML (1½ CUPS) WHITE WINE

750 ML (3 CUPS) CHICKEN STOCK

Preheat the oven to 160°C. To make the sauce, put the tomatoes and garlic in a large roasting tin, then drizzle with half the olive oil and season with sea salt and freshly ground black pepper. Roast the tomatoes, uncovered, for 1 hour.

Meanwhile, to make the meatballs, put the mince in a bowl and add the onions and eggs. Soak the breadcrumbs in the water for 5 minutes, then add to the mince. Add the parsley and season well with salt and pepper. In a circular motion, rub the ingredients together, then set aside while you finish the sauce.

In a large heavy-based pot, cook the onions in the remaining olive oil on a medium heat, without colouring, until soft. Toss the roasted tomatoes and garlic into the pot with the onions. Add the wine and bring to the boil for 5 minutes, then add the stock. Reduce the heat and simmer for 1 hour.

Transfer the tomato mixture to a food processor (or use a stick blender) and blend. Return the tomato sauce to the stove. Bring to the boil and simmer for a further 10 minutes, stirring occasionally. Season generously with salt and pepper.

When the sauce is ready, wet your hands and form the mince mixture into walnut-sized balls, then place the meatballs into the tomato sauce. Once the sauce is boiling again, cover and simmer for 30 minutes, stirring occasionally. Serve with crusty bread and a salad, or with a pasta such as fettucine.

Serves 8

Felicia Kahn

Growing up, I don't remember ever seeing a bought biscuit in the house. My mother, a renowned biscuit maker, ensured there were never less than ten varieties in our biscuit tin at any time. My grandfather was a well-known cheese maker, winning awards in the Netherlands and around the world. This, and the fact that my mum was always in the kitchen, whet my appetite for all things food related.

I married Stanley, a real 'meat and potato man' (his background was cattle breeding and potato farming!), and together we opened The Rawhide, a steakhouse in Johannesburg. So it was no surprise that we ended up in the catering business when we immigrated to Australia in 1986. We started at the Bondi Hadassa butchery, revolutionising the kosher food industry with cooked foods and smallgoods. Soon after, Front Page Catering was born, which later merged to become Passion8, the largest kosher caterer in Australia. We've seen generations of families grow, quietly witnessing their Bar Mitzvahs, weddings and births of their children, all the while supplying them with the most delicious food!

These are our most popular sweet treats to serve with coffee, and one of my favourites. Each year we make at least 10 000 of these delectable morsels!

CHOCOLATE ALMOND FLORENTINES

250 ML (1 CUP) PURE CREAM
  (35% FAT)
115 G (⅓ CUP) HONEY
240 G SUGAR
350 G (4 CUPS) FLAKED ALMONDS
200 G BEST-QUALITY DARK,
  MILK OR WHITE CHOCOLATE,
  ROUGHLY CHOPPED

Preheat the oven to 130°C. Grease and line a rectangular baking tray (33 x 25 cm, and at least 5 mm deep).

In a large saucepan, heat the cream, honey and sugar on a low heat and bring to the boil. Continue to cook, swirling the pan occasionally, until the mixture becomes frothy and dark caramel in colour (about 15 minutes), or until it reaches 130°C (266°F) on a sugar thermometer. Stir in the almonds and pour into the prepared tray. When cool enough to handle, flatten the mixture with your hands, pressing into the base and corners of the tray. Bake for 45 minutes, or until the almond slab is golden brown. While warm, score into triangles or squares.

Melt the chocolate in a double boiler or in a heatproof bowl over a saucepan of simmering water. Once the almond slab is cool, snap it along the score lines and dip one half of each florentine into the chocolate. Place on baking paper to harden. Store in the fridge in an airtight container.

Makes about 45 florentines

Venetia Kalinko

One of the first memories of my childhood in South Africa is of my mother, busy in the kitchen, pickling olives and turnips; she was a wonderful cook. As a young child I showed no interest in cooking, but over the years, I have become a truly passionate cook. Perhaps I learnt from my mother by osmosis!

From the first day of married life, I have kept a kosher kitchen, and continue my search for the perfect dairy-free dessert to enjoy after a meat meal. We have travelled widely, and my love for good food has been enhanced by visiting exotic and wondrous places, then returning and trying to replicate the dishes we ate.

There is no greater joy for me than setting a beautiful table, arranging the flowers and then preparing a feast to share with the people I love. I believe if you cook with passion, the food tastes so much better.

Whenever my husband and sons were told they were having chicken for dinner, this was the dish they wanted. This recipe was inspired by Rhona Walhaus' 'chicken rouge', from the early seventies in Cape Town. I have added my own touches to the recipe over the years, often adding parboiled potatoes halfway through the cooking time.

MY OWN 'RED CHICKEN'

75 G (½ CUP) PLAIN FLOUR
1 TEASPOON SWEET PAPRIKA
2 MEDIUM CHICKENS, EACH
   CUT INTO 8 PIECES
OIL, FOR FRYING

SAUCE
1 TABLESPOON BROWN SUGAR
1 TEASPOON TABASCO SAUCE
200 ML TOMATO SAUCE (KETCHUP)
2 TEASPOONS WORCESTERSHIRE
   SAUCE
250 ML (1 CUP) WATER
2 TEASPOONS DIJON MUSTARD
1 TABLESPOON SOY SAUCE
125 ML (½ CUP) WHITE VINEGAR
2 ONIONS, FINELY SLICED

Preheat the oven to 200°C. Place the flour, paprika and salt and freshly ground black pepper in a large plastic bag. Add the chicken pieces and toss to coat well.

Heat the oil in a large frying pan on a high heat. Shake off the excess flour and fry the chicken pieces in batches until crisp and brown on both sides. Place in an ovenproof dish.

Combine all the ingredients for the sauce and pour over the chicken. Cover with the lid or foil and bake for 30 minutes, then uncover and bake for a further 30 minutes, or until the chicken is cooked through and the sauce is reduced. Serve with risoni, rice or potatoes.

Serves 8–10

This has been an all-time family favourite for over thirty years. It may look time-consuming and complicated, but really it isn't, and it's worth taking the extra bit of time to achieve an authentic Indian curry. This is my basic curry recipe, which I also use to make oxtail curry, substituting the oxtail for the lamb chops.

TRADITIONAL INDIAN LAMB CURRY

12–16 LAMB FOREQUARTER CHOPS
  (CUT TO DOUBLE THICKNESS)
100 ML PEANUT OIL
3 ONIONS, CHOPPED
2 CLOVES GARLIC, CRUSHED
2 X 800 G TINS CRUSHED
  TOMATOES
800 ML WATER
1–2 TEASPOONS SALT, OR TO TASTE
6 POTATOES, PEELED AND
  QUARTERED
400 G TIN CANNELLINI BEANS
  AND/OR 400 G TIN CHICKPEAS,
  RINSED AND DRAINED

MUSLIN SPICE BAG
30 CM SQUARE PIECE OF MUSLIN
1 BUNCH CORIANDER
1 BUNCH PARSLEY
3 STALKS FRESH CURRY LEAVES
1 HEAPED TABLESPOON PANCH
  PHORA (SEE NOTE)
2 STAR ANISE

SPICE MIX
1 TABLESPOON GROUND CORIANDER
1 TABLESPOON GROUND CUMIN
½ TEASPOON CHILLI FLAKES
1 TEASPOON GROUND CARDAMOM
1 TEASPOON GROUND CINNAMON
½ TEASPOON GROUND GINGER
1 TEASPOON GROUND TURMERIC
1 TABLESPOON GARAM MASALA

Preheat the oven to 180°C. To make the spice bag, cut off the leafy sections of both bunches of herbs and place in the middle of the muslin along with the curry leaves, panch phora and star anise. Roll up and secure the ends with string. Mix all the spice mix ingredients together in a bowl.

Season the lamb chops well with salt. Heat 1 tablespoon of the peanut oil (per batch) in a large cast-iron pot or flameproof casserole dish on a medium–high heat and brown the lamb chops in small batches. Set the lamb chops aside on a plate. In the same pot, add 2 tablespoons peanut oil and sauté the onions until translucent. Add the garlic and cook for 1–2 minutes, then add the spice mix and stir for 2–3 minutes, or until aromatic. Add the tomatoes, water, salt and the muslin spice bag. Simmer for a few minutes.

Return the chops (with any juices that may have accumulated on the plate) to the pot and bring to the boil. Place the pot in the oven and cook for 2 hours, or until the chops are very tender. After 1 hour 15 minutes, add the potatoes, beans and/or chickpeas. Serve with rice.

Serves 6–8

Note: Panch phora is a five-spice mixture made from ground cumin, nigella, mustard, fenugreek and fennel seeds. It is sold in specialist spice stores and Indian grocery stores.

Sharon Katz

In all the houses I've lived, I can clearly remember one room — the kitchen, and it was always filled with people cooking together, chatting and eating.

It started with my grandmother, Serena. I never met her but I've visited her tiny village in Romania and have shared incredible meals with her relatives — my relatives. The meals always started with chopping and carrying wood, fetching and boiling water, catching and killing a chicken, and drinking many glasses of homemade schnapps. All ingredients were either picked fresh from the garden or taken from glass jars stored in deep, cool cellars. My great-aunts made the finest noodles for the chicken soup and the flakiest pastry for the fruit tarts; they milked the cows and made their own butter and cheese. There was not a packet in sight!

My mother was born amid a group of aunts and neighbours in the middle of the harvest season. The next day she was slung over her mother's shoulder and given a piece of muslin filled with rum-soaked poppyseeds to suck on as they returned to harvest the crops. One generation later it was a completely different story, when my mother found herself here in Australia and gave birth to me, alone, while my father waited outside. She had no family to support her, and being new to the country had no community. She brought with her the memories of the food she ate as a child, but no recipes.

Shortly after I was born, Kati, our new housekeeper, walked into our home and took over the kitchen. Because she came from a very similar part of the world, she re-created the food that was so familiar to my mother. Now, her recipes are ours. As I grew up, I would beg my mother to miss school so I could stay in the kitchen with Kati and help her cook, listen to her stories and lick the bowls, wooden spoons and whisks. Even today as a grown woman with my own children, I still love to hear her call out to my mum, 'kesz a puliszka!' — the polenta's ready! We sit down with a pot of steaming yellow polenta, a bottle of full-cream milk and a jar of plum povidl on the table. We eat and talk and laugh — a lot. Four generations of us, just like back in the village.

These are more like a rolled pastry than a biscuit. Kati still makes them for us, and happily makes several hundred whenever there is a wedding or party. She used to put both the plum and walnut ones in a huge pile on the same dish and it would be a lottery as to which was which. We'd bite into one and then, depending on which type we'd picked, swap it, because some of us liked plum and others walnut.

PLUM AND WALNUT KIFLI

DOUGH
250 G CREAM CHEESE, AT ROOM
    TEMPERATURE
250 G UNSALTED BUTTER, AT ROOM
    TEMPERATURE
2 EGG YOLKS
2 TABLESPOONS CASTER SUGAR
350 G (2⅓ CUPS) PLAIN FLOUR

FILLINGS
FOR THE WALNUT FILLING, COMBINE:
100 G (¾ CUP) GROUND WALNUTS
FINELY CHOPPED ZEST OF 1 LEMON
2 TABLESPOONS CASTER SUGAR

FOR THE JAM FILLING:
1 JAR (½–1 TEASPOON FOR EACH
    TRIANGLE) POVIDL (PLUM JAM)

ABOUT 160 G (1 CUP) VANILLA
    ICING SUGAR (SEE NOTE), FOR
    DUSTING

Start this recipe the day before. Put the dough ingredients in a bowl and mix with your hands to make a soft dough. Divide into eight balls, wrap each one well in plastic wrap and place in the freezer overnight. Before you are ready to use, defrost the dough at room temperature.

Preheat the oven to 160°C. Line two large baking trays.

Using one ball at a time, roll out thinly on a well-floured board into a 20–22 cm diameter circle. Cut into 8 triangles, like a pizza. Put half a teaspoon of filling in the middle of the base of the triangle, fold over to cover, then roll towards the point of the triangle. Place on the prepared trays and bend the ends down to make a crescent shape. Repeat for all the triangles. Bake for 30–40 minutes until golden. When cool, roll in vanilla icing sugar. Store in an airtight container with any excess vanilla icing sugar tipped on top of the biscuits.

Makes 64 biscuits

Note: To make vanilla icing sugar, scrape the seeds from a vanilla bean into 1 kg icing sugar mixture in a container. Roughly chop the vanilla bean and add to the icing sugar. Shake vigorously until the seeds are dispersed, using a whisk to help if needed. Seal the container until ready to use. Lasts for months.

These two quite different kifli (loosely meaning 'biscuit') recipes came from Kati, who was given the recipes by her mother's mother in (the former) Yugoslavia. She has now passed them on to me and my children. The almond kifli are a delightfully buttery, nutty and crumbly biscuit, perfect with a cup of tea.

ALMOND KIFLI

125 G WHOLE RAW ALMONDS
  (SKIN ON), FRESHLY GROUND
  (IN A FOOD PROCESSOR)
250 G UNSALTED BUTTER, AT ROOM
  TEMPERATURE
350 G (2⅓ CUPS) PLAIN FLOUR
1 TABLESPOON VANILLA (CASTER)
  SUGAR (SEE NOTE)
ABOUT 160 G (1 CUP) VANILLA
  ICING SUGAR (SEE NOTE,
  PAGE 149), FOR DUSTING

Preheat the oven to 160°C. Line two large baking trays.

Mix together the ground almonds, butter, flour and vanilla sugar by hand until a dough is formed, taking care not to overwork the dough. This can also be done in a food processor. Roll the dough into small thumb-sized rolls and bend slightly into crescent shapes. Place on the prepared trays and bake for 30–40 minutes until pale golden. When cool, roll in the vanilla icing sugar. Store in an airtight container with any excess vanilla icing sugar tipped on top of the biscuits.

Makes 60 biscuits

Note: To make vanilla (caster) sugar, store a split vanilla bean (it can be one from which the seeds have been removed for another dish) in 1 kg caster sugar in a container. Shake vigorously and allow the vanilla flavour to permeate for at least 1 week before using. Seal the container until ready to use. Lasts for months.

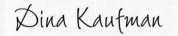

Dina Kaufman

The food of my childhood was an interesting blend of my heritage — Israeli and Iraqi. My mother was such a great cook and baker of cakes that she actually never allowed me into the kitchen! Saturday lunch at Mum's was unforgettable. The whole family gathered around a table laden with sides and mains, salads and fruits, homemade ice creams and, of course, the essential sweets and cakes. Lunch always finished late in the evening, when we would all head home carting boxes of leftovers.

I started cooking later in life. The first recipe I ever mastered was cheese blintzes (thanks to my sister-in-law!), and soon I discovered I had quite a passion for baking. I moved to Sydney and, needing recipes for traditional festival foods, Mum worked through every one of her treasured recipes, measuring and checking each ingredient before passing them on to me. Now I pass them to my daughters.

Originally Mum's filling for these crumb cookies was povidl *(plum jam), and then at Purim time she would spread them with chocolate and cut the pastries into triangles for* hamantashen. *These are my daughters' favourites.*

MUM'S CRUMB COOKIES

DOUGH
375 G (2½ CUPS) PLAIN FLOUR
2 TEASPOONS VANILLA SUGAR
   (SEE NOTE, PAGE 150)
2 TEASPOONS BAKING POWDER
200 G UNSALTED BUTTER, AT ROOM
   TEMPERATURE
2 EGGS
110 G (½ CUP) SUGAR

FILLING
500 G PITTED DRIED DATES
⅛ TEASPOON GROUND CLOVES
80 ML (⅓ CUP) HOT WATER
2 TEASPOONS HONEY

ICING SUGAR, TO SERVE

Grease and flour (or line) a 33 x 23 cm baking tin.

To make the dough, mix all the dough ingredients together, preferably in a food processor, until it forms a soft dough. Divide the dough into two parts: two-thirds and one-third. Put the smaller portion in the freezer for 2–3 hours. Press the remaining two-third portion of dough into the base of the prepared tin so it is evenly distributed.

Preheat the oven to 200°C. To make the filling, place all the filling ingredients in a food processor and process until a paste is formed. Spread evenly on the base dough. Using the coarse side of a grater, grate the frozen dough over the filling. Bake for 20–25 minutes, or until the crumbs become golden. Allow to cool and then cut into diamonds or squares. Sprinkle with icing sugar before serving. Keeps well in an airtight container.

Makes 18

Variations: Other filling options include 320 g (1 cup) povidl (plum jam); 250 g chocolate-hazelnut spread; 4 granny smith apples, grated and mixed with 120 g (6 tablespoons) sugar, finely grated zest of 1 lemon and 1 teaspoon ground cinnamon.

Melanie Knep

Food is a link that connects us to the past, enduring long after our loved ones have passed on. Some of my warmest memories of my childhood in South Africa were also my mother's happiest times. We would have 'freezer days', when we spent the day together in her kitchen, preparing all our family favourites, such as chicken soup, crispy little perogen, blintzes and cakes, which were then ready to be defrosted whenever guests dropped by.

I too love my time in the kitchen, sometimes with my daughter, Lauren, by my side, and there is no greater joy than when my family sit around my table and truly enjoy what I have prepared.

I sadly remember my mother dying, but the opportunity to record our treasured family recipes ensures that I now remember her standing in the kitchen, living.

Lauren Fink

Some of my fondest childhood memories of growing up in Pretoria were the times I spent in my granny's kitchen. She was a wonderful cook and the kitchen was always a hive of activity. My mother, Melanie, is a fabulous cook, and my father's German heritage gave me a real appreciation for delicious European flavours. With all these great influences around me, how could I not love food and cooking?!

My parents, brother and I moved to Sydney in 1979 — one of the earliest young South African families to make a home here in beautiful Sydney. We came without extended family, but the incredible welcome from our local community and the weekly invitations to Shabbat dinners really helped ease us into this new life.

When I got married my mother gave me a set of Women's Weekly cookbooks with all the basics that I needed to know. I remember being so excited about them. Who would have thought all these years later we would be creating our own cookbook!

Now with my own family of five, food is still central to our lives. We love eating out at great restaurants, and mealtimes at home are what always bring us all together. Although my cooking is very simple and often starts without a recipe, I really would love to pass my mum's and my family recipes on to my children. What a great legacy that would be.

Lauren

There is no real story behind this delicious cheesecake other than it is an old South African recipe. The original version came from Dorryce Rock, the sister of one of my dearest friends. It's really easy; in fact, my youngest daughter now makes it on her own. This recipe has top priority when I entertain on Sunday afternoons.

SOUTH AFRICAN CHEESECAKE

250 G (1 PACKET) PLAIN SWEET
    BISCUITS, SUCH AS MARIE
250 G UNSALTED BUTTER, MELTED
6 EGGS, SEPARATED
230 G (1 CUP) CASTER SUGAR
500 G LIGHT (PHILADELPHIA)
    CREAM CHEESE
250 G (PHILADELPHIA) CREAM
    CHEESE
200 ML PURE CREAM (35% FAT)

Preheat the oven to 180°C. You will need a deep 31 x 28 cm baking dish.

To make the cheesecake base, put the biscuits in a food processor and process, then combine with the melted butter. Press the mixture evenly into the base of the dish.

Beat the egg yolks until light and fluffy, adding the sugar gradually. Add the cream cheese, one-third at a time, and beat on high speed to ensure there are no lumps. Slowly add the cream and beat until smooth.

In a separate bowl, whisk the egg whites until stiff peaks form. Fold the cream cheese mixture into the egg whites, one-third at a time, then pour the mixture over the cheesecake base. Bake for 50 minutes until golden brown and slightly wobbly. Serve at room temperature.

Serves 12

I really believe that if a restaurant serves a great salad, then you know you are in the right place. A few years ago I was having lunch at Barney Greengrass in Los Angeles and ordered a salad, while my husband, Bruce, tucked into an onion bagel topped with lox, eggs and onions. I was feeling a little envious ... but then my tuna salad arrived and it was fantastic. I wrote down what I thought was in it, and when I got back home I tried to re-create it. Of course it was nothing like what I'd eaten there, but it was still delicious.

LAUREN'S TUNA SALAD

500 G MIXED LETTUCE LEAVES,
   SUCH AS ICEBERG, COS, BUTTER
   LETTUCE, RADICCHIO AND
   MACHE, FINELY CHOPPED
160 G BABY CAPERS, RINSED AND
   DRAINED
250 G ROASTED CAPSICUM IN OIL,
   DICED
235 G (1½ CUPS) SHELLED FRESH
   GREEN PEAS, BLANCHED
3 BUNCHES ASPARAGUS, BLANCHED
   AND CUT INTO 1 CM PIECES
650 G GOOD-QUALITY TINNED
   TUNA IN OIL, DRAINED AND
   WELL FLAKED
125 ML (½ CUP) WHITE BALSAMIC
   VINEGAR
125 ML (½ CUP) OLIVE OIL

Put all the ingredients, except the vinegar and oil, in a bowl and use your hands to toss everything together.

Season generously with sea salt and freshly ground black pepper and dress with the balsamic vinegar and olive oil.

Serves 6

Melanie

We often ate herring while we were growing up. Chopped herring was a regular on our Shabbat table, always served with kichel. We loved the salty fishy and vinegar flavour of the herring with the crisp and slightly sweet kichel. I used to watch my mother make the kichel and it was really a labour of love. My job was to watch the oven — with such a short cooking time, they burned easily if you got distracted. Then I progressed to rolling and cutting the diamond shapes. When I immigrated to Sydney I wanted to keep up the tradition, but never had recipes for either the herring or kichel, so I searched through all our Jewish cookbooks and created simple versions that reminded me of my mother's.

CHOPPED HERRING AND KICHEL

CHOPPED HERRING

4 MAATJES HERRING FILLETS,
  SOAKED IN WATER FOR 1 HOUR,
  THEN RINSED WITH COLD WATER
  (OR 2 SALTED WHOLE HERRINGS,
  SOAKED OVERNIGHT, SKINNED
  AND BONED)
1 APPLE, PEELED AND CORED
4 PLAIN SWEET BISCUITS, SUCH
  AS MARIE
1 HARD-BOILED EGG
¼ ONION
WHITE VINEGAR AND SUGAR,
  TO TASTE

KICHEL

3 LARGE EGGS
1½ TABLESPOONS VEGETABLE OIL
1 TEASPOON SUGAR
GOOD PINCH OF SALT
225 G (1½ CUPS) PLAIN FLOUR
EXTRA FLOUR, FOR ROLLING
EXTRA OIL, FOR BRUSHING
EXTRA SUGAR, FOR SPRINKLING

TO MAKE THE CHOPPED HERRING

In a mincer, mince the herrings together with the apple, biscuits, egg and onion. Season well with vinegar and sugar to taste. You need to be able to strongly taste both the vinegar and sugar, but neither should be overpowering. Serve with the kichel.

Serves 6

TO MAKE THE KICHEL

Preheat the oven to 250°C. Grease a large baking tray.

Beat the eggs, oil, sugar and salt until well amalgamated. Add the flour, a little at a time, to form a very wet and soft dough (a thick batter consistency). Add more flour if necessary.

Flour a board very well. Use the extra flour to make the piece of dough workable and to ensure it doesn't stick. Take a small piece of dough and roll it out with a rolling pin, until 1–2 mm thick. It should be as thin as you are able to roll it, without tearing. Brush the surface of the dough lightly with the extra oil and sprinkle lightly with extra sugar. Using a pizza cutter, cut into 6 cm diamonds and place on the baking tray. The dough scraps, even though they are covered with oil and sugar, can be gathered up and rolled again.

Bake for about 4 minutes, or until light golden. Repeat with the remaining dough. Cool well before placing in an airtight container. Keeps for up to 3 months.

Makes about 125 kichel

Melanie

This is my mother's version of cheese blintzes. She always made them then froze some, so that whenever anyone popped in she could pull them out of the freezer, pour over some cream and bake them, then serve delicious 'freshly made' blintzes. Another way of preparing them is to make a bigger parcel from each crepe (with 2 generous tablespoons of filling in each), fold over with the short ends tucked in, and fry gently in butter until the filling is cooked and the outside is golden.

CHEESE BLINTZES

CREPES
3 EGGS
625 ML (2½ CUPS) WATER
225 G (1½ CUPS) PLAIN FLOUR
PINCH OF SALT
½ TEASPOON BAKING POWDER

CREAM CHEESE FILLING
2 EGGS
500 G FULL-FAT CREAM CHEESE, AT
    ROOM TEMPERATURE
4 TABLESPOONS CASTER SUGAR,
    OR TO TASTE
2 TABLESPOONS SOUR CREAM,
    OR AS NEEDED

300 ML PURE CREAM (35% FAT)
CINNAMON SUGAR, TO SERVE
EXTRA SOUR CREAM, TO SERVE
    (OPTIONAL)

To make the crepes, beat the eggs and water together. Sift the flour, salt and baking powder together, then add to the egg mixture and beat until smooth. The batter needs to be of a thin pouring consistency; if necessary add more water. Allow the batter to rest while you make the filling.

To make the filling, beat together the eggs, cream cheese and sugar. Beat in the sour cream (enough to make a smooth paste). Taste for sugar and add more if needed. It should be just sweet.

To cook the crepes, heat a non-stick crepe pan or 20 cm frying pan and grease lightly. Pour enough batter into the pan to thinly coat the base, swirling the pan so the batter spreads to the edge, and tip off any excess. Cook the crepe on one side only until it is dry, comes away from the side of the pan and is very lightly coloured. Tip out onto a paper towel, with the uncooked side facing downwards – this will be the inside of the blintz. Continue with the rest of the batter, piling the crepes on top of each other. Repeat to make 18–20 crepes.

Preheat the oven to 200°C. Grease a large baking dish.

To assemble the blintzes, place a crepe on the work surface, uncooked side upwards. Put 1–2 tablespoons of cream cheese filling in the centre. Fold one side over and then the other to form a roll. Fold one end over onto the top and the other end underneath, to form a square parcel. Place the blintzes in the dish, snugly, side by side. Pour the cream over so there is about 7–8 mm of cream in the bottom of the dish. You may need some extra cream depending on the size of your dish. Bake for about 30 minutes, uncovered, or until the blintzes are golden brown and puffed up. Sprinkle with cinnamon sugar and serve with sour cream on the side if desired.

Makes 18–20 blintzes

Zina Komonski (Nan Babes)

As this book is written, I am a proud 96 year old. I live by myself and still love to cook! My family were Russian, but were living in Harbin, China, when I was born in 1914. Later, while we were living in Shanghai, the Communist occupation made life extremely difficult for Jews; luckily for us, with no passports or money to our name, the Jewish Agency sponsored our move to Israel in 1949.

In Israel, life was different. We didn't have the food I so fondly associated with my childhood in China, nor the borscht and piroshky of my Russian ancestors, but we loved Middle Eastern comfort foods like soups and stews, often made with barley. In 1957 we immigrated to Australia, and our Russian, Chinese and Israeli influences came with us, as well as the beautiful silver candlesticks that I remember my mother lighting every Friday night.

When we were living in Israel, my daughter Susie used to eat sugared peanuts made by our neighbour. She loved them so much she went next door and asked how to make them — and then taught me! When I moved to Australia, I started making them with almonds, often giving them as gifts.

NANA'S NUTS

55 G (¼ CUP) SUGAR
60 ML (¼ CUP) WATER
180 G (1 HEAPED CUP) RAW
    ALMONDS

You will need two baking trays, preferably non-stick.

Put the sugar and water in a cast-iron or heavy-based saucepan on a low heat, and stir to dissolve the sugar. Add the almonds. Once the liquid starts to bubble, shake and stir continuously until the liquid has evaporated and sugar crystals have formed on the almonds. Keep stirring and separating the almonds, and moving them around the pan until there are no more crystals on the almonds and they are shiny. This will take 10–15 minutes.

Tip the almonds onto one of the trays, taking care as they are very hot. Working quickly, separate each almond using a spoon, and transfer it onto the other tray. When cool enough to touch, separate any almonds that have stuck together. Once cooled, store in an airtight jar.

Makes about 1 heaped cup

Pastilla is a delectable prune and walnut log that is perfect on its own or as an accompaniment to cheese. This is an old Russian Jewish recipe from my great-great-grandmother, which was passed down to me. Several years ago, my friend Jan Nash tasted my pastilla and asked me for the recipe, which I gladly gave her. Her version is now known as 'Pastilla Nash' and sells all over the world. And I still make it for my family!

PASTILLA

800 g (3⅔ cups) pitted prunes, minced (see note)
600 g (2¾ cups) sugar
2 teaspoons honey
2 teaspoons lemon juice
400 g (4 cups) walnuts
125 g (1⅓ cups) desiccated coconut

Put the prunes and sugar in a very large saucepan and mix together with a splash of water until combined into a sludgy mixture. Cook on a medium heat until the sugar is dissolved. Add the honey and lemon juice and cook for about 15 minutes until the mixture becomes a very thick jam that sticks to the side of the pan. Test if it is ready by putting a bit on a spoon and placing it in the fridge – it should go hard after a few minutes. Add the walnuts and cook for a further 5–10 minutes, stirring.

Spread the coconut over two boards or trays. Place tennis ball-sized spoonfuls of the mixture onto the coconut. When cool enough to handle, roll each mound into a sausage shape, so it becomes a smooth log covered in coconut. Wrap in foil and refrigerate until cold. Slice thinly on the diagonal to serve. Keeps well.

Makes 15 logs

Note: For the best results, the prunes should be minced in a mincer.

Angelique Lazarus

Sandwiches with sambal oelek, peanut butter and cucumber were my favourite lunchbox fillers for school in the early 1970s and definitely gave me an interesting start-up as a foodie. Eating and drinking were a huge part of our family life. My Indonesian Dutch father was a chef. We spent many days at home enjoying the Indonesian rijsttafel — our table groaning under platters of nasi goreng, fried pisang (banana), satays of different kinds, with many exotic rice and vegetable dishes — shared with countless family members and eased down with copious quantities of beer and wine.

I was born in Melbourne, but at the age of eight, my family moved to Holland, my mother's home country. From there we lived in Belgium before returning to Perth. This must have instilled wanderlust in me; I left Australia in my teens and travelled extensively around the world, before meeting my husband, David, in London. He whisked me off to Zimbabwe, then Johannesburg and then, to complete yet another circle, we moved back to Australia, this time to Sydney, with our three children. And here we are staying!

My exceptional mother-in-law, Miriam, took me under her wing and taught me every little thing I needed to know to be a good wife to her son. She taught me the basics: how to look after the home, how to set a table, how to follow the Jewish way of life and, best of all, she instilled in me a love for her traditional Lithuanian food. She is a fabulous cook and we have spent many an hour together in the kitchen. Her legacy will undoubtedly continue as she has now taken our daughter Mia under her culinary wing, too.

I was taught to make this cake by my youngest son's godfather. He is a restaurateur in Johannesburg and Cape Town and this carrot cake is one of their signature cakes. Over the years I have adapted the recipe, adding a few of my own touches. The cake is addictive and whenever I offer to make something for someone, this is always their first request.

CARROT CAKE

DRY INGREDIENTS
375 G (2½ CUPS) PLAIN FLOUR
2 TEASPOONS BAKING POWDER
1½ TEASPOONS BICARBONATE OF
   SODA
2 TEASPOONS GROUND CINNAMON
½ TEASPOON GROUND NUTMEG
½ TEASPOON ALLSPICE
2 TEASPOONS SALT

WET INGREDIENTS
345 G (1½ CUPS) CASTER SUGAR
375 ML (1½ CUPS) VEGETABLE OIL
4 EGGS

FRUIT
475 G (3 CUPS) GRATED CARROT
140 G (½ CUP) DRAINED TINNED
   CRUSHED PINEAPPLE
200 G (1⅔ CUPS) CHOPPED PECANS

GLAZE
2 TABLESPOONS VEGETABLE OIL
110 G (½ CUP) BROWN SUGAR
2 TABLESPOONS MILK
40 G CHOPPED PECANS (OPTIONAL)

ICING
250 G CREAM CHEESE, AT ROOM
   TEMPERATURE
125 G UNSALTED BUTTER, AT ROOM
   TEMPERATURE
500 G ICING SUGAR
1 TEASPOON VANILLA EXTRACT

Preheat the oven to 180°C. Grease a large 26 cm x 10 cm deep angel cake tin.

Sift the dry ingredients together into a bowl. In a separate bowl, beat the wet ingredients together until frothy. Mix together the dry, wet and fruit ingredients. Pour the mixture into the prepared tin and bake for 35 minutes.

While the cake is baking, mix together the glaze ingredients in a saucepan and heat until just combined.

Remove the cake from the oven and pour the glaze over the cake while it is hot. Return the cake to the oven for 15 minutes, or until a skewer inserted into the cake comes out clean.

To make the icing, beat together the cream cheese, butter, icing sugar and vanilla. When the cake is completely cool, turn it out of the tin and set on a serving plate, glazed side up. Spread the icing generously over the cake.

Serves 12

The Levins

Elza Levin

I inherited my mother's love of baking and my granny's love of cooking. Granny's house (in Johannesburg, South Africa) was the gathering point for my entire family and as a young girl I adored helping her prepare the most beautiful feasts.

It was through my training as a preschool teacher that I really learnt how to cook. Our meticulous cooking teacher insisted that everything be just so, even her tea tray had to be set out perfectly, the tea, milk and sugar lined up in exactly the correct order. In 1951 I married my childhood sweetheart, Lynton, and we had four children. He loved life, family and his food — simple dishes like roast meats and potatoes, but cakes were his absolute favourite.

Sadly, Lynton passed away, but I am so thankful to have such an incredible family — my children and their spouses, nine grandchildren and two beautiful great-granddaughters (so far!) — who all love nothing better than to sit around the table together, eating and chatting. This is surely the best thing in life!

Judy Lowy

I come from a family who love to cook, bake, eat and gather together. When I was young, my mum, Elza, was always entertaining and I loved helping her. Over the years Mum and I have really enjoyed sharing our love of cooking — going to classes, swapping cookbooks and recipes, and chatting about new dishes, new ingredients and great chefs. We have created treasured family rituals with three generations of the family coming together twice a year for our 'herring-making day' and 'jam-making day'.

My sister-in-law, Roz, made it her mission to teach me all the basics when I lived with her as an eighteen year old. I think of her every time I clean a chicken! When I was living in New York as a newlywed, I craved my mum's cooking and I would often call home to ask her to dictate recipes to me over the phone.

Over time my love of cooking has grown, fuelled mainly by my love of eating! We are so very lucky in Sydney to have the best produce at our fingertips. It is one of my favourite things in the whole world to invite family and friends over to share great food and wine, and linger at the table for hours.

Elza

I learnt how to make chicken soup from my granny Fanny, who came from Lithuania. She cooked traditional Jewish food very well and taught me many things, but her specialty was her soup and kreplach, which she made for us all the time, and which I now make for my grandchildren. If making kreplach at the same time, add 4 pieces of beef marrow bone with meat (or 2 pieces beef top rib) to the soup ingredients. I sometimes also add a couple of sprigs of dill.

FANNY'S CHICKEN SOUP

2 KG CHICKEN WINGS

1.5 KG CHICKEN FRAMES

500 G CHICKEN GIBLETS

1 LEEK, WHITE PART ONLY, CLEANED AND CUT IN HALF

4–6 CARROTS, PEELED AND LEFT WHOLE

2 PARSNIPS, PEELED AND CUT INTO CHUNKS

1 SWEDE, PEELED AND CUT INTO CHUNKS

½ BUNCH CURLY PARSLEY

1 TABLESPOON SALT, OR TO TASTE

1 TABLESPOON PEPPER, OR TO TASTE

Start this recipe one day ahead. Put all the ingredients in an extra large (at least 12–15 litre) stockpot. Cover with cold water and bring to the boil, skimming constantly. Turn the heat down and simmer for 3–4 hours, always skimming the scum until it is clear. If the liquid reduces too much, top up with more water.

Allow to cool. Strain the soup, reserving the carrots for serving. (If making kreplach and you have added the beef, reserve the meat from the meat bones, a few giblets and the leek.) Discard everything else. Refrigerate overnight. The next day, remove the fat from the top of the soup. Reheat to serve, and taste for seasoning. Serve with kreplach and lokshen.

Makes 5–6 litres clear soup; it freezes well

Elza

These are a type of Jewish–style meat ravioli that are traditionally served in chicken soup at the Friday night Shabbat meal. Lokshen, egg noodles, are often served with it as well.

KREPLACH AND LOKSHEN

FILLING
300 G MEAT FROM THE SOUP
   BONES
A FEW GIBLETS FROM THE SOUP
COOKED LEEK FROM THE SOUP
1 EGG, BEATEN

DOUGH
2 EGGS
½ TEASPOON SALT
150 G (1 CUP) PLAIN FLOUR

To make the filling, mince the meat, giblets and leek, or chop them very finely. Mix the egg into the meat mixture and season generously with salt and pepper.

To make the dough, lightly beat the eggs and salt in a bowl. Add the flour gradually until you have a soft dough.

Using a pasta machine, start on the widest setting and roll the dough through, using a little flour if necessary, until you are on about the second narrowest setting. The dough needs to be thin, but not paper-thin.

Lay out the rolled dough on a floured surface and place 1 teaspoon of filling on the dough at intervals along the middle (lengthwise), leaving space around each mound to seal. Moisten the dough with a little water or beaten egg. Fold the dough over the filling so that one side has a fold and the other will be a join of the two sides. Using a cookie cutter or a glass, cut out a semicircle. Press down on the edges, making sure each one is sealed properly. The scraps can be re-used either as more kreplach, or as lokshen.

Bring a large pot of well-salted water to the boil. Add the kreplach and cook for 10 minutes, or until soft. Drain. To serve, reheat in the soup for a few minutes.

Makes 3–4 dozen kreplach

TO MAKE THE LOKSHEN (EGG NOODLES)
Use the dough ingredients and roll to the same thickness. Either cut into thin strips or roll through the linguini or fettucine setting of the pasta machine. Cook for a few minutes only in plenty of boiling salted water.

Judy

After Steven and I first married, we lived in New York for a while. We often visited the then-famous Cafe des Artistes, which was well known for its gravalax. I was given their wonderful recipe by a friend and have served it to break the fast on Yom Kippur ever since. Use the very freshest salmon or ocean trout.

GRAVALAX WITH DILL AND MUSTARD SAUCE

1 WHOLE SALMON (2–3 KG), CUT
   INTO 2 LARGE FILLETS, SKIN ON
   AND BONES REMOVED
80 ML (⅓ CUP) VODKA
2 BUNCHES DILL, BROKEN INTO
   SPRIGS
100 G (⅓ CUP) COARSE SALT
75 G (⅓ CUP) SUGAR
2 TABLESPOONS LIGHTLY CRUSHED
   BLACK PEPPERCORNS (PUT IN A
   SNAP-LOCK BAG AND BASH WITH
   A ROLLING PIN)

DILL AND MUSTARD SAUCE
1½ TABLESPOONS WHITE WINE
   VINEGAR
1¾ TABLESPOONS SUGAR
125 ML (½ CUP) OLIVE OIL
100 G DIJON MUSTARD
1 TABLESPOON CHOPPED DILL
1 HEAPED TABLESPOON GROUND
   WHITE PEPPER, OR TO TASTE
1 HANDFUL DILL SPRIGS, FOR
   GARNISH
LEMON WEDGES, TO SERVE

You will need a ceramic or glass baking dish large enough to hold the two salmon fillets. Dry the salmon fillets with paper towel, then sprinkle the vodka all over the salmon. Spread one-third of the dill in the bottom of the dish. Combine the salt, sugar and peppercorns and sprinkle some of the mixture on each side of both fillets, reserving some.

Place one fillet skin side down on the dill, spread another one-third of the dill over the top, then place the other fillet on top, skin side up. You will now have salmon skin on the top and bottom of the stacked fillets. Sprinkle the remaining salt mixture and remaining dill over the top. Cover with plastic wrap.

Place a large platter or chopping board on the fillets and weight them down with heavy cans. Place in the fridge and leave to marinate for at least 24 hours (up to 36 hours), turning the salmon over every 12 hours. The fish will release some liquid.

To make the dill and mustard sauce, whisk the vinegar and sugar together until the sugar is dissolved. Slowly add the olive oil, whisking well until the oil is incorporated. Blend in the mustard and chopped dill and season with the white pepper to taste. Cover and refrigerate until needed.

Remove the weights, plastic wrap and dill. Using paper towel, wipe off all the seasoning mixture. At this point you can freeze the salmon for easy slicing, or serve immediately. When you are ready to serve, slice the salmon very thinly on the angle, starting at the narrow end. Serve with the dill and mustard sauce, lemon wedges, and sourdough toasts, pumpernickel or rye bread.

Each fillet serves 8–10 as a starter or more as part of a buffet

Judy

Many years ago, Marieke Brugman, one of Australia's great chefs and cooking teachers, taught a version of this pear dish to a group of us on a weekend cooking retreat. These pears are incredibly sweet and rich, and from the slow-cooking process they have a unique texture akin to a pear purée — but still retaining their pear shape.

SLOW-ROASTED PEARS

440 G (2 CUPS) SUGAR
500 ML (2 CUPS) WATER
250 ML (1 CUP) WHITE WINE
5 DRIED BAY LEAVES
1 VANILLA BEAN, SPLIT
6 BROWN PEARS (BEURRE BOSC),
  PEELED AND LEFT WHOLE

Combine all the ingredients, except the pears, in a saucepan large enough to fit all the pears standing upright in a single layer. Bring to the boil. Add the pears, ensuring they are all submerged. It is useful to cover them with baking paper and place a plate on top that won't squash the pears, but will gently keep them submerged. Simmer, covered, for 1 hour.

Remove the lid and continue to simmer on a very low heat (the lowest setting possible) for 3 hours until the juices reduce to a syrupy caramel, basting the pears carefully from time to time. The pears can also be cooked in the oven on 150°C for 3 hours after the first hour on the stovetop. Serve with ice cream or crème fraîche.

Serves 6

Judy

I learnt to make this fabulous tarte tatin years ago from Marieke Brugman, at the beautiful Howqua Dale gourmet retreat in the Victorian high country. It has become one of my staples and I have never tasted a better one anywhere in the world.

PEAR TARTE TATIN

8–9 BROWN PEARS (BEURRE BOSC)
100 G COLD UNSALTED BUTTER
220 G (1 CUP FIRMLY PACKED)
   BROWN SUGAR
JUICE OF 1 LARGE LEMON
1 TABLESPOON POIRE WILLIAM
   LIQUEUR
CASTER SUGAR, FOR SPRINKLING

PASTRY
240 G PLAIN FLOUR
200 G UNSALTED BUTTER
125 G SOUR CREAM

Start this recipe the day before. Peel, halve and core the pears. Slice each half in thick slices on the diagonal, lengthwise and not quite all the way through, keeping each half together at the stem end. Meanwhile, melt the butter in a large ovenproof frying pan or skillet, approximately 30 cm in diameter.

Arrange the sliced pear halves in the pan, then scatter the brown sugar and then the lemon juice over the top. Simmer on a medium heat for about 1 hour until the juices have thickened and are well caramelised. Towards the end of cooking, sprinkle over the liqueur. Knowing when you have cooked the pears sufficiently is a very important step. If you peek under one of the pears it should be golden brown and the juices will start to have the smell of caramel rather than sugar. Cool and refrigerate in the pan.

To make the pastry, combine the ingredients in a food processor just until it forms a ball. Cover and refrigerate no longer than 30 minutes. Preheat the oven to 200°C.

Roll out the pastry to a disc large enough to fit over the pan. Gently lift the pastry on, to cover the cooked and cooled pears, and tuck in the edges so that they will form a lip later when inverted. Sprinkle the top with a little caster sugar. (You can refrigerate the tart at this point for up to 24 hours.) Bake for 40–50 minutes, or until the pastry is cooked and golden. With extreme care, up-end the tart onto a serving dish large enough to contain it. Serve immediately.

Serves 10–12

Elza

I took an interest in cake decorating some years ago, and have since started making special birthday cakes for family and close friends. It is truly a labour of love, as it takes hours and hours to make the intricate characters and designs that my grandchildren seem to want. The cake I almost always use is this chocolate cake, which I have been making for almost twenty years. It is an easy cake to make and never fails to impress.

CELEBRATION CHOCOLATE CAKE

250 G UNSALTED BUTTER

200 G DARK CHOCOLATE, ROUGHLY CHOPPED

1 TABLESPOON INSTANT COFFEE DISSOLVED IN 375 ML (1½ CUPS) HOT WATER

460 G (2 CUPS) CASTER SUGAR

185 G (1¼ CUPS) SELF-RAISING FLOUR

75 G (½ CUP) PLAIN FLOUR

30 G (¼ CUP) BEST-QUALITY COCOA POWDER

2 EGGS

2 TEASPOONS VANILLA EXTRACT

Preheat the oven to 150°C. Grease and line the base and side of a 24 cm springform cake tin.

Melt the butter in a saucepan on a low heat and add the chocolate, stirring to melt. Add the coffee and water mixture and sugar, stirring to dissolve.

Remove the pan from the heat, stir to combine and pour into a large mixing bowl. Cool for 5 minutes. Sift the flours and cocoa into the chocolate mixture and stir through. Add the eggs and vanilla and combine with an electric mixer until smooth.

Pour the mixture into the prepared tin. Bake for 1½ hours, or until the cake is cooked through (this is a very moist cake). The top will be crusty and cracked. If you prefer a smoother top, cut a piece of baking paper the size of the cake top and place it on top of the mixture before baking.

Serves 10

The Meyerowitz sisters

Food has always been central to our lives. We were blessed to have two wonderful grandmothers, Sadie and Cela. One made 'pure' vegetable soup for the vegetarian grandchildren – with just a bit of chicken for flavouring – and the other put cucumbers on her eyes and home-grown crushed strawberries on her face, and at the same time had a firm belief that both chocolate and Coca-Cola were good for growing children!

Jane Grossberg

I was the first of the three sisters to arrive in Sydney. I visited my best friend here in the late 1980s, met and fell in love with Ian, and shortly after immigrated and married. We are blessed with two children and I thank my lucky stars that both my sisters now live down our road. I think of myself as a rondaawel – a little round thatched hut – a person that can never be cornered. I am a holistic thinker, broad minded and free spirited, and that is reflected in my cooking. I married into a family whom I adore, whose waking question is 'What's to eat?' and where it was absolutely necessary to become a good cook to be a part of it.

Cathy Milwidsky

I was the next to arrive, in the late 1990s, when, despite some exciting times in Johannesburg (we married the week Mandela was released from prison), things began to change and living in South Africa with two little girls became scary. Sydney is now well and truly home. I love my work as Director of Moriah College preschools, and I love to cook. I enjoy simple, easy food made with the freshest ingredients and I am so lucky my husband has such excellent barbecuing skills!

Nicky Sepel

I arrived last of the three, with my husband and three daughters. We were so fortunate to already have a warm supportive family in Sydney, so our arrival and life here was instantly happy. Like my sisters, I love to cook, having taken my inspiration from our grandmother, Cela. I make cinnamon bulkas every year to break the fast at Yom Kippur, reminding us all of the times back in South Africa when we would bake together.

These delicious cinnamon buns were originally made by our family friend Irene. We always make them when a baby in our family is born. As the mum goes into labour, so the dough is made; the baby is born into a cinnamon-infused world of warm, soft, sweet buns. There are many different ways of rolling the dough: our mum, Barbie, likes to make the cinnamon buns into a large celebration babke — *a spectacular way to mark a special occasion.*

IRENE'S BULKAS (CINNAMON BUNS)

DOUGH

1 x 7 G SACHET DRIED YEAST

125 ML (½ CUP) WARM WATER
(HALF BOILING, HALF COLD)

3 TEASPOONS CASTER SUGAR (FOR
YEAST)

665 G (4½ CUPS) PLAIN FLOUR

115 G (½ CUP) CASTER SUGAR

1 TEASPOON SALT

100 ML PURE CREAM (35% FAT)

50 ML MILK

2 EGGS

85 G UNSALTED BUTTER

2 TABLESPOONS VEGETABLE OIL

220 G (1 CUP) SUGAR

2 TABLESPOONS GROUND
CINNAMON

2 EGG YOLKS

1 TABLESPOON WARM WATER

125 G UNSALTED BUTTER, MELTED

SESAME SEEDS, FOR SPRINKLING
(OPTIONAL)

To make the dough, mix together the yeast, warm water and 3 teaspoons caster sugar in a small bowl. Cover and set aside for about 20 minutes, or until the yeast is frothy. In a very large bowl, mix together the flour, ½ cup caster sugar and salt. In a separate bowl, beat the cream, milk and eggs. Melt the butter in a small saucepan, then stir in the oil. Alternatively, melt the butter in a heatproof jug or bowl in the microwave.

Make a well in the flour mixture and add the frothy yeast mixture and then the other two liquid mixtures. Mix it all together with a wooden spoon until combined, then knead for a minute or two until it comes together as a dough. Cover very snugly with a warm towel or blanket, place in a warm draught-free area and allow to double in bulk before kneading. This may take 2 hours, depending on the weather. Place on a lightly floured board and knead well for 10 minutes until you have a very smooth, slightly sticky dough (see note).

TO MAKE THE BULKAS

Preheat the oven to 180°C. Line a baking tray or a deep cake tin (square or round) with baking paper. Combine the sugar and cinnamon in a bowl. Lightly beat the egg yolks and warm water together in a separate bowl and set aside.

Divide the dough into three equal pieces, each about 400 g. Place one piece of dough on a floured board and roll into a large rectangular shape, about A4 (28 x 21 cm) in size. Brush with 1–2 tablespoons of the melted butter until well covered. Sprinkle generously with 1–2 heaped tablespoons of the cinnamon sugar. Roll up loosely, starting at the long side, to form a 28 cm log. Trim the ends. Repeat with the remaining two pieces.

Using a sharp knife, cut each log into six equal pieces. Turn each onto its side on the baking tray, so that the snail pattern is facing upwards. Press down on the snail with the heel of your hand and flatten slightly to make a nice scroll. If you want them to join while baking, place each scroll about 1 cm apart; if you prefer individual and separate buns, place them well apart on the tray.

Brush the egg glaze over the buns and sprinkle with sesame seeds if desired. Allow to rise again for at least 10 minutes, then bake for 20 minutes, or until golden and cooked through.

Makes 18 buns

TO MAKE BARBIE'S CELEBRATION BABKE

Grease and flour an angel cake tin. Divide the dough into six equal pieces, each about 200 g. Place one piece on a floured board and roll into a rectangular shape slightly smaller than an A4 page, about 3 mm thick.

Brush with 2 tablespoons of the melted butter and sprinkle with 3–4 heaped teaspoons of the cinnamon sugar. Roll up, starting at the short end, so you have a fat 20 cm log. Stand the roll up on its end, put it vertically in the tin and squash down slightly. Repeat with the remaining balls of dough until the cake tin is snugly filled. Brush with the egg glaze and sprinkle with sesame seeds if desired. Allow to rise again for 10 minutes, then bake at 180°C for 40 minutes, or until cooked through.

Note: The dough can be refrigerated or frozen before or after the rise. You can also let it rise, make your buns/babke, then refrigerate in the tin until ready to bake. Bring to room temperature for several hours before rising, kneading or baking.

Cathy

This is a recipe from our grandmother Sadie. It is a South African tradition to serve the crispy perogen floating in the chicken soup. I love making Cela's chicken soup and Sadie's perogen on Rosh Hashanah — so when our children eat it, they have something from each great-grandmother.

PEROGEN

2 TABLESPOONS OLIVE OIL

2 SMALL BROWN ONIONS, CHOPPED

2 CLOVES GARLIC, CRUSHED

SPRIG OF ROSEMARY

PINCH OF SALT

500 G BEEF MINCE

200 ML RED WINE

400 G TIN PEELED TOMATOES

1 TABLESPOON TOMATO PASTE

1½ TABLESPOONS TOMATO SAUCE
   (KETCHUP)

1 TABLESPOON KECAP MANIS
   (SWEET SOY SAUCE)

1 TABLESPOON WORCESTERSHIRE
   SAUCE

1.2 KG BEST-QUALITY PUFF PASTRY

Heat the olive oil in a large heavy-based saucepan. Cook the onions on a low heat until soft and glassy, then add the garlic, rosemary and salt. Continue to stir until fragrant and soft. Add the mince and brown well, then add all the other ingredients (except the pastry) and cook for a further 5 minutes, stirring from time to time.

Using a stick blender, blend the meat mixture in the saucepan to create an even consistency. Cook for a further 10 minutes, or until most of the liquid has evaporated. Remove from the heat and cool to room temperature.

Preheat the oven to 180°C. Line a large baking tray. You may need to bake the perogen in batches.

If using block puff pastry, roll it out on a well-floured surface to a 3 mm thickness (or place the puff pastry sheets on the work surface). Using a cookie cutter or small glass (7–8 cm in diameter), cut out circles from the pastry. Place one teaspoon of the meat filling onto one half of each circle and fold the other side over to create a small half-moon shape. Using a fork, press down around the edges to seal. Place the perogen on the prepared tray and bake for 20–30 minutes until crisp and golden. Serve as an accompaniment to chicken soup or on their own as a tiny 'meat pie'.

Makes 80 perogen

Note: The perogen can be filled and then placed into lined containers and frozen until ready to bake and serve.

Cathy

This Asian-style fish is what connects us to our new life in Australia — broadening our palates to embrace flavours from the East. This recipe combines Asian flavours with a method for cooking fish that we learnt while on holidays in Portugal many years ago.

ASIAN-STYLE SNAPPER

1 x 2.5 KG WHOLE SNAPPER (OR
   OCEAN TROUT, RED EMPEROR),
   BUTTERFLIED
CORIANDER LEAVES, FINELY
   CHOPPED, TO SERVE

MARINADE
2 TABLESPOONS PEANUT OIL
2 TABLESPOONS OLIVE OIL
JUICE OF 3 LIMES
FINELY GRATED ZEST OF 1 LIME
1 STALK LEMONGRASS, BOTTOM
   THIRD AND TENDER LEAVES
   ONLY, VERY FINELY CHOPPED
4 CM KNOB OF GINGER, GRATED
1 BUNCH CORIANDER, STALKS AND
   ROOTS ONLY, CLEANED AND
   CHOPPED
1–2 LARGE RED CHILLIES, SEEDED
   AND CHOPPED
60 ML (¼ CUP) LIGHT SOY SAUCE
60 ML (¼ CUP) KECAP MANIS
   (SWEET SOY SAUCE)
1 TABLESPOON GRATED PALM
   SUGAR OR BROWN SUGAR

Put all the marinade ingredients in a heavy-based saucepan on the stovetop and simmer, covered, on a low heat for around 30 minutes, or until the marinade thickens.

Preheat a barbecue to hot. Put the fish on the barbecue, flesh side down, and cook for about 10 minutes, or until a crust forms on the underside. Using two large slides, turn the fish over so it is now cooking with the skin side down. Cook for a further 5 minutes, or until the fish is just cooked at the thickest part. Place on a serving plate and while it is hot, pour over the hot marinade. Garnish with the coriander.

Serves 6–8

Nicky

Chocolate is synonymous with memories of our grandmother Cela. My most vivid ones are of us making chocolate mousse together, licking the bowl while at the same time she begged and pleaded with us to glug down an ampoule of bee pollen to supplement and enhance our nutrition!

CHOCOLATE MOUSSE

200 G BEST-QUALITY DARK
    CHOCOLATE (70% COCOA IS
    IDEAL), CHOPPED
8 EGGS, AT ROOM TEMPERATURE,
    SEPARATED
1 TEASPOON VANILLA EXTRACT
    (OPTIONAL)
GRATED CHOCOLATE, FOR
    DECORATION

Melt the chocolate in a double boiler or in a heatproof bowl over a saucepan of simmering water, stirring with a wooden spoon until smooth. Remove from the heat and cool for 5 minutes, or until just warm to the touch. It is important to take the time to allow it to cool properly. If it is too hot the egg yolks will cook, if it is too cold the mixture will seize.

While the chocolate is cooling, beat the egg whites until soft peaks form. In a separate bowl, beat the egg yolks with a fork. Stir one spoonful of melted chocolate into the egg yolks (not the other way around or it will seize) and beat until completely blended. Continue to add the chocolate to the egg yolks, a spoonful at a time, stirring after each addition, until all the chocolate has been beaten into the yolks.

Using a metal spoon, carefully and gently fold the egg whites into the chocolate mixture until it is incorporated. Fold through the vanilla if desired. Pour into a glass bowl or individual serving glasses and decorate with grated chocolate. Cover with plastic wrap and refrigerate for at least 8 hours before serving.

Serves 8

Jane

Our grandmother Cela studied in Vienna, loving not only the new culture but the wonderful pastries. It was there that she learnt how to craft this amazing and unique apple strudel. We all have wonderful memories of her standing in her best silk dress, hair coiffed and with rings on every finger of her left hand (the right hand was clear for kneading), making this strudel. The dough takes some practice, but it is so much fun! Be prepared for a kitchen covered in flour and apples, but you will be rewarded with the most delicious strudel you have ever tasted.

CELA'S APPLE STRUDEL

DOUGH
300 G (2 CUPS) PLAIN FLOUR
1 EGG
1 TEASPOON CASTER SUGAR
1 TABLESPOON VEGETABLE OIL
PINCH OF SALT
185 ML (¾ CUP) WARM TAP WATER

FILLING
125 ML (½ CUP) VEGETABLE OIL
650 G (3 CUPS) SUGAR
50 G GROUND CINNAMON
400 G WALNUTS, BROKEN UP OR
    WHOLE
330 G (2 CUPS) SULTANAS
15 GOLDEN DELICIOUS OR GRANNY
    SMITH APPLES, PEELED, GRATED
    AND DRAINED FOR 20 MINUTES,
    THEN JUICE SQUEEZED OUT
ICING SUGAR, FOR DUSTING

Preheat the oven to 200°C. Put two small to medium saucepans (with heatproof handles) in the oven to heat.

To make the dough, place the flour in a mound on a work surface and make a well in the centre. Crack the egg into the well, then sprinkle the sugar, oil and salt onto the egg. With a small knife, beat them together in the well. Slowly add 125 ml (½ cup) of the water, or more as needed, and incorporate the surrounding flour until you have a ball of sticky dough. Flour the work surface. Using the heel of your hand, knead the dough by folding the piece in half towards you and pressing the hand away from you into the dough. Turn a quarter turn anticlockwise and repeat. Knead for 5 minutes until you have a firm but slightly sticky dough.

Take one of the hot saucepans from the oven and sit it over the dough, to cover it. When the saucepan cools (after about 5 minutes), exchange it for the other hot pan (return the cooled saucepan to the oven to reheat). Continue this for 20 minutes, or until the dough is soft, warm and elastic. Meanwhile, place a clean tablecloth on a table and flour it very well.

Place the dough on a well-floured board and roll out until it is a large oval, about 40 x 30 cm. Lift the dough up and put it over your entire arm so it can stretch down and increase in size, until it is about four times the original size. Carefully put the dough on the tablecloth. Quickly pull the edges out so the dough stretches and becomes translucent, like tissue paper (it is easier with two people). Don't worry if holes appear, but try to avoid them where possible. Cut off any dried or thick edges.

TO ASSEMBLE THE STRUDEL

Line an extra large baking tray with baking paper. Sprinkle 60 ml (¼ cup) of the oil over the dough on the tablecloth, gently spreading it across the surface with your hands. To make the filling, combine the sugar and cinnamon and sprinkle it over the dough, followed by the walnuts and sultanas and then the apple, making sure you have squeezed out all the juice.

Using the tablecloth, roll the strudel up into a huge long sausage. Carefully roll the sausage onto the prepared tray. Using your hands, spread the remaining oil onto the outside of the strudel. Bake for 45 minutes, or until golden brown. When cool, sprinkle with icing sugar.

Serves 20

Molly Moses

Bombay was a peaceful place to grow up, and my family enjoyed the affections of both our Hindu and Muslim neighbours. As the eldest daughter of ten children, I learnt my most valuable lessons helping my mother with all her household duties. The traditional food of our Baghdadi (Jewish) Indian community consisted of hot curries and mild pilaus, delicious chutneys and pickles, all manner of flatbreads, and fragrant rosewater and cardamom sweets. Our Shabbat dinners were always rustic mouth-watering banquet-style feasts where formalities were kept to a minimum and anyone was welcome. Things were kept simple and enjoyment was found in both the colourful tapestry of the food on the table and the company around it.

In the mid-1960s we immigrated to Australia in search of a brighter future for our children. I came to Sydney with my husband, daughter and siblings, and my parents followed soon after. I was often nostalgic for all the foods from home, because it was a reflection of where I came from and who I was. Although I never had any formal training in cooking, I found just by thinking about the times I'd stood beside my mother in the kitchen — watching, tasting and helping — that I could remember the different spices and flavours needed to re-create the dishes of my childhood.

By virtue of leaving India and migrating to a new world, my family was exposed to a variety of new influences and cultures. As we spread our wings, my own family became a mini United Nations, adopting and absorbing people from all around the world. This recipe is from Jenny, my Indonesian sister-in-law, who is a wonderful cook. Of course our mutual love of chilli and spice meant that there was no need to 'acquire' a taste for Indonesian food, just a need to learn how to make it! With its winning combination of chilli, fresh garlic and tomato paste, this dish is literally bursting with flavour — but it's not for the faint-hearted.

MASALA CHILLI FISH

80 ML (⅓ CUP) VEGETABLE OIL
3 LARGE ONIONS, FINELY CHOPPED
1 TABLESPOON TOMATO PASTE
125 ML (½ CUP) WATER
750 G FIRM WHITE FISH FILLETS,
    SUCH AS BLUE EYE TREVALLA,
    CUT INTO SMALL PIECES
60 ML (¼ CUP) LEMON JUICE

MASALA SPICE MIX
1 TEASPOON CRUSHED GARLIC
1 TEASPOON GRATED FRESH GINGER
1 TEASPOON CURRY POWDER
1 TABLESPOON GROUND CUMIN
1 TABLESPOON GROUND CARAWAY
    SEEDS
1 TABLESPOON CHILLI PASTE OR
    A HANDFUL OF CHILLIES MADE
    INTO A PASTE

To make the masala spice mix, put the ingredients in a bowl and mix well.

Heat the oil in a frying pan and fry the onions until golden brown. Add the masala spice mix and cook for 2 minutes, stirring. Add the tomato paste and stir for a few minutes, then stir in the water to make a sauce. Cook the sauce for a further 5 minutes and then season with salt to taste.

Immerse the fish in the sauce and cook gently, tossing from time to time, for 10 minutes, or until almost cooked through. Add the lemon juice and season with salt. Remove the pan from the heat and let rest for a few minutes. Serve on turmeric-roasted potatoes (page 200) or steamed basmati rice.

Serves 4–6

Chitarnee, a sweet and sour dish with onion sauce, is a dish unique to the Baghdadi Indian community. Whenever she was able, my mother made sure to cook this for us on Friday night, as it was the one day of the week we were able to buy meat or chicken, a rare luxury in those days. The sheer quantity of onions ensures that the dish is imbued with a rich sweetness, which is balanced by the sharp burst of vinegar thrown in at the end, making this dish quite unique.

BEEF CHITARNEE

1 KG BLADE OR CHUCK STEAK
125 ML (½ CUP) VEGETABLE OIL
1 KG ONIONS, FINELY CHOPPED
1 RED CAPSICUM, FINELY CHOPPED
½ TEASPOON SALT
1 TEASPOON GRATED FRESH GINGER
1 TEASPOON CRUSHED GARLIC
2 TABLESPOONS GROUND CORIANDER
2 TEASPOONS GROUND CUMIN
1 TABLESPOON PAPRIKA
1 TEASPOON GARAM MASALA
½ TEASPOON GROUND TURMERIC
½ TEASPOON BLACK PEPPER
500 G RIPE TOMATOES, CHOPPED
140 G TOMATO PASTE
1 TABLESPOON SUGAR
80 ML (⅓ CUP) BROWN VINEGAR
6 FRESH CURRY LEAVES

Cut the beef into 5 cm pieces and set aside. Heat the oil in a frying pan and fry the onions, capsicum and salt on a medium heat for 10–15 minutes until the onions are golden brown. Add the ginger and garlic and cook for a few minutes, stirring.

Add the meat and all the spices and brown the meat well. Add the tomatoes and tomato paste and cook for about 2 hours, or until the meat is tender. Stir through the sugar, vinegar and curry leaves and cook for a further 5 minutes. Serve with turmeric-roasted potatoes.

Serves 4–6

TURMERIC-ROASTED POTATOES

1 KG DESIREE OR PONTIAC
   POTATOES, PEELED AND
   QUARTERED
½ TEASPOON GROUND TURMERIC
2 TABLESPOONS VEGETABLE OIL

Preheat the oven to 220°C. Boil the potatoes and turmeric in salted water for 5 minutes, then drain off the water. Cover with the lid and shake the potatoes vigorously to rough the surfaces a little. Put the potatoes in a greased baking dish. Heat the oil in the oven in a heatproof jug for 5 minutes, then pour it over the potatoes. Bake for 40 minutes, tossing the potatoes occasionally, until crisp and golden. Sprinkle with salt.

Serves 4–6

It was the delicate aroma of cardamom and garam masala wafting out of my Muslim neighbour's home every Friday that lured me into asking for this recipe. This one-pot dish is akin to a chicken biryani, but milder on the palate and very lightly spiced. This is a great dish to serve to people who are not accustomed to eating spicy food but want to sample a taste of the East. An interesting addition is to top it with roasted pine nuts, almonds and raisins.

CHICKEN PERSIAN PILAU

400 G (2 CUPS) BASMATI RICE

140–160 ML VEGETABLE OIL

1 CHICKEN, CUT INTO 8 PIECES

2 LARGE ONIONS, FINELY CHOPPED

1 HEAPED TEASPOON GRATED
    FRESH GINGER

1 HEAPED TEASPOON CRUSHED
    GARLIC

1 HEAPED TEASPOON GROUND
    TURMERIC

2 HEAPED TEASPOONS GARAM
    MASALA

½ TEASPOON FRESHLY GROUND
    BLACK PEPPER

2 TEASPOONS SALT

375 ML (1½ CUPS) CHICKEN
    STOCK OR WATER

1 KG CARROTS, PEELED AND
    GRATED

6 HARD-BOILED EGGS, SLICED,
    FOR GARNISH (OPTIONAL)

Cook the rice in boiling salted water for 8–10 minutes, then, when almost cooked, drain and set aside.

In a large frying pan, heat 1–2 tablespoons of the oil and brown the chicken pieces until dark golden. Remove and set aside. In the same pan, fry the onions in 60 ml (¼ cup) of the oil until golden brown. Add the ginger, garlic, spices and 1 teaspoon of the salt. Cook for a few minutes, stirring. Add the chicken stock and stir the onions and spices to make a spiced stock. Remove 250 ml (1 cup) of the liquid and reserve. Return the chicken pieces to the pan and set aside.

Preheat the oven to 180°C. In a large flameproof casserole dish, heat 60 ml (¼ cup) of the oil and fry the carrots and remaining 1 teaspoon of salt for 10 minutes, or until soft. On top of the carrots, layer the chicken pieces and spiced stock from the pan. Cover with the cooked rice and then pour the reserved liquid on top of the rice. Season with a little more salt. Cover and bake for 50 minutes, or until the chicken is cooked through and the rice is steaming on top. To serve, garnish with the sliced boiled eggs if desired.

Serves 4–6

The Musries

Myrtle

Myrtle was well known for her Jewish Iraqi food and loved dishes like hamim, kuba *and fish curries. Saturday lunches were always a special time, with the smell of slow-cooked* hamim *permeating the house.*

Home was Bombay, India, where she lived with her five siblings and parents until marrying David. Myrtle never cooked as a youngster, as there was always someone working in the kitchen. But after she was married, her Iraqi-born mother-in-law visited regularly, teaching her to cook 'Baghdad style'.

The Musries moved to Sydney in 1966 with their three young children. Myrtle spent much of her time cooking and entertaining, often asking friends for advice on recipes. She lived the last decades of her life enjoying her two great passions: fashion design and food. Her children fondly remember Myrtle in the kitchen, and replicate many of her dishes — a beautiful inheritance.

Abe

I ate my first chilli at the age of three and started cooking as soon as I was allowed. I was mesmerised by the flavours and smells of my Indian and Iraqi heritage, and was heavily influenced by my late mum Myrtle's style of cooking. I've always used plenty of fresh herbs and a lot of heat! One of my warmest memories is of Mum showing me how to mix different spices together and teaching me to create amazing rich curries from a bunch of simple ingredients.

Along the way I have influenced my wife and two children's palates and now they too crave the spicy dishes of my youth.

Dahl is a traditional dish from Bombay, India. Growing up there, this meal was usually prepared and eaten on a Thursday night, a tradition that was handed down from generation to generation of Sephardi Jews. Meat was only a small part of the Sephardi diet and enjoyed on Shabbat, so there were many vegetarian meals eaten during the week.

MYRTLE'S DAHL

200 G RED LENTILS, RINSED
1 LITRE (4 CUPS) WATER
1 TEASPOON SALT
1 TEASPOON GROUND TURMERIC
4 FRESH CURRY LEAVES
1 TABLESPOON OLIVE OIL
2 ONIONS, FINELY CHOPPED
1 TEASPOON GROUND CUMIN
1 TEASPOON GRATED FRESH
   GINGER
1 TEASPOON CRUSHED GARLIC
PINCH OF SALT
1 TABLESPOON TOMATO PASTE
1 TOMATO, CHOPPED
1 HANDFUL CHOPPED CORIANDER
   LEAVES

Put the lentils in a saucepan with the water, salt and turmeric and bring to the boil. Cover and simmer for 40–50 minutes, or until the lentils are tender. Add the curry leaves and set aside.

Heat the olive oil in a frying pan on a medium heat and cook the onions for about 15 minutes, or until soft and golden brown. Add the cumin, ginger, garlic and salt. Fry for a few minutes, then add the tomato paste and tomato and cook for about 5 minutes until the tomato softens.

Add the lentils and simmer for a further 5–10 minutes until thickened. Season with salt to taste. Rest for 5 minutes for the flavours to infuse, then sprinkle with coriander to serve.

Serves 8 as a side dish

Shiftas are made from minced beef (or sometimes fish) mixed with fresh herbs and spices, which are then rolled and lightly grilled or barbecued. They are usually accompanied by an aromatic coriander and mint sauce known as hulba. *Serve with a green salad or quinoa tabbouleh (page 68).*

ABE'S BEEF SHIFTAS WITH HULBA

SHIFTAS

1 KG PREMIUM (PREFERABLY NOT
    LEAN) BEEF MINCE
1 BUNCH CORIANDER, LEAVES AND
    STEMS, FINELY CHOPPED
½ BUNCH MINT, LEAVES ONLY,
    FINELY CHOPPED
1 ONION, FINELY CHOPPED
2 TEASPOONS GROUND CORIANDER
1 TEASPOON GROUND CUMIN
JUICE OF ½ LIME
CHOPPED LARGE GREEN CHILLI,
    TO TASTE
2 TABLESPOONS OLIVE OIL
1 TEASPOON SALT

HULBA (GREEN SAUCE)

3 BUNCHES CORIANDER, LEAVES
    AND STEMS, CHOPPED
1 BUNCH MINT, LEAVES ONLY,
    CHOPPED
1 TEASPOON SALT
JUICE OF ½ LIME
1 BIRD'S EYE CHILLI, SEEDED
    AND CHOPPED
60 ML (¼ CUP) OLIVE OIL
60 ML (¼ CUP) WATER
1 TABLESPOON GROUND
    FENUGREEK (OPTIONAL)

To make the shiftas, put all the shifta ingredients into a large bowl and mix together. Roll into thumb-sized sausages and allow to rest in the fridge for at least 1 hour.

Meanwhile, to make the hulba, put the coriander, mint, salt, lime juice, chilli and olive oil in a blender. Add enough of the water to just moisten (you may not need it all), and blend to form a sauce consistency. If the sauce is too thin or watery, add the fenugreek to thicken. Cover and set aside.

When you are ready to cook, heat the barbecue to a low–medium heat and cook the shiftas for 10 minutes, turning frequently, or until cooked through. Serve with the hulba.

Makes about 50

Maxine Pacanowski

My love of food began early in life. I clearly remember visiting my great-grandparents' pickling factory in Marrickville, Sydney, which they ran from the back of their house. I recall the thrill I felt as a small child seeing their yard crammed with giant timber vats bursting with pickled onions; my mouth still waters as I remember their wonderful flavour and pungent sweet smell.

My passion for cooking and eating well came from my English aunty Annie, the matriarch of our family. As a child I used to love watching her cook. Her kitchen was constantly bustling, with beautiful smells wafting out, and there was always so much good food to eat. She was forever preparing something wonderful and entertaining with such joy and love. She absolutely inspired me to do the same.

I don't remember the origin of this, my husband's favourite cake, but I have been making it for more than thirty years. It is also delicious if you toss some fresh or frozen berries through the apple slices.

CINNAMON AND APPLE PIE

6–8 GRANNY SMITH APPLES, PEELED AND SLICED
1½ TABLESPOONS CINNAMON SUGAR
3 EGGS
345 G (1½ CUPS) CASTER SUGAR
375 ML (1½ CUPS) LIGHT OLIVE OIL OR VEGETABLE OIL
3 TEASPOONS VANILLA EXTRACT
225 G (1½ CUPS) PLAIN FLOUR
EXTRA CINNAMON SUGAR (OPTIONAL), FOR SPRINKLING

Preheat the oven to 180°C. Grease and line the base and side of a 26 cm springform cake tin.

Layer the apple slices in the prepared tin so they come about two-thirds of the way up the side. Sprinkle the cinnamon sugar over the apples.

Make a batter by beating the eggs and sugar until light and fluffy. Add the oil and vanilla and beat well, then stir in the flour. Spoon the batter on top of the cinnamon-covered apples and sprinkle with extra cinnamon sugar if desired. Bake for 1 hour 20 minutes, or until a skewer inserted into the cake comes out clean. Cool in the tin. Serve warm with cream or ice cream.

Serves 10

Carol Pryer

Cooking has been a major part of my life, both from a home and work perspective. My family originated in Vienna and perhaps that is where my interest began — Austria is surely home to some of the best bakers and cooks in the world. Sadly, my parents were forced to leave their home, as rising anti-Semitism made life extremely difficult in the late 1930s. They lived in Shanghai for eight years, then ended up in Sydney.

My mother and mother-in-law always cooked beautifully and most of my cooking skills were gleaned from them.

I love trying recipes from other people, sometimes experimenting and altering them to suit my own style. I am particularly fastidious, always carefully measuring and weighing everything to make sure what I did the first time is the same as the tenth. I just like to be certain that my recipes, which I will pass on to my daughters, will always work out.

This is a moist and seriously chocolatey cake. The recipe came from a cafe we used to own in Darlinghurst, Cafe Dov. It came with the cafe, and my daughters, who have inherited my cooking passion, perfected it. It was freshly made each and every day and was so popular that it was often hard to keep up with the demand!

FLOURLESS CHOCOLATE CAKE

10 EGGS, SEPARATED
500 G BEST-QUALITY DARK
   CHOCOLATE, ROUGHLY CHOPPED
300 G (1⅓ CUPS) CASTER SUGAR
300 G UNSALTED BUTTER, CHOPPED
200 G (2 CUPS) GROUND ALMONDS
   (ALMOND MEAL)

Preheat the oven to 180°C. Grease and line the base and side of a 28 cm springform cake tin.

Whisk the egg whites until stiff peaks form, then set aside. Melt the chocolate, sugar and butter in a double boiler or in a heatproof bowl over a saucepan of simmering water. Once melted, stir thoroughly to combine. Remove the chocolate mixture from the heat and allow it to cool a little, then mix in the ground almonds.

Beat the egg yolks into the chocolate mixture, a little at a time. Stir two spoonfuls of the egg whites into the chocolate mixture to lighten it, then gently fold in the remaining egg whites. Pour into the prepared tin and bake for 40–50 minutes, or until cooked through. Allow to cool before removing from the tin.

Serves 12–14

Sophie Rose

To me, family is food and food is family. Our family banquet table is Sephardic, with very strong Spanish and Middle Eastern influences, paying respect to my father's Egyptian roots and homage to my mother's Venezuelan heritage. When my husband joined the family, he adjusted to our banquet and then adjusted his belt!

In our family everything must be done from scratch. We spend at least four days cooking for any festival and the reward is then sitting down, eating and not leaving the table for a very long time. For Rosh Hashanah we make an abundance of date-filled and other delicious biscuits to symbolise our wish for a sweet new year. The Pesach family breakfast is a highlight and lasts almost all day. We make bimuelos, a fried sweet matzo dumpling coated in the syrup from charoset. As they are cooked, we sit and enjoy a progressive breakfast, then roll home happily late in the afternoon.

Based on a recipe from Solomon's Matzo Meal, I make these at Passover when we don't eat anything with flour in it. I make a mountain of them, then spend a day driving around to drop them off as presents for family and friends. I often replace the almonds with a different fruit and nut mix — date and walnut is our family favourite.

PASSOVER ALMOND BREAD

4 EGG WHITES
1 EGG YOLK, BEATEN
150 G SUGAR
1 TABLESPOON VEGETABLE OIL
150 G WHOLE ALMONDS
150 G SUPERFINE MATZO MEAL

Preheat the oven to 180°C. Grease a 26 x 9 cm loaf tin.

Beat the egg whites until stiff peaks form. Add the egg yolk, then the remaining ingredients slowly and mix well. Pour into the prepared tin and bake for about 30 minutes, or until firm and lightly golden. Remove from the tin and allow to stand overnight, or for at least 6 hours.

Preheat the oven to 180°C. Slice the loaf into very thin slices and place flat on ungreased baking trays. Bake for 10–12 minutes, or until lightly browned and crisp. Remove from the trays and cool on wire racks before storing in an airtight container.

Makes about 40

Marny Rosen

Cooking has always been my passion, which started when I was a young girl growing up in South Africa. From the age of ten, I was baking and experimenting, learning along the way by trial and error, picking up recipes and tips from friends and always asking questions from the chefs in restaurants that I loved.

Both my mum, with her Lithuanian background, and step-mum, with her Scottish roots, have always been really wonderful and particularly creative cooks. Amazingly, it was my Lithuanian grandfather who taught my grandmother how to cook all the traditional Ashkenazi dishes, which were then passed down to me via my mother. I remember sitting on the kitchen counter as a little girl, watching my mother and my granny Bella cook and marvelling at how they could each turn simple ingredients into something so special.

This dish came together simply by combining ingredients that I love. This is not one of those potato salads that is heavily laden with dressing — less mayonnaise is used rather than more — it's a wonderful fresh dish with a light dressing. This has become my signature salad, which friends often ask me to make. And then everyone asks me for the recipe!

ROASTED BABY POTATO SALAD WITH CAPERS

2 KG MIXED BABY POTATOES
    (WITH A VARIETY OF SHAPES
    AND COLOURS)
80 ML (⅓ CUP) OLIVE OIL
2 TABLESPOONS SALT
1 BUNCH SPRING ONIONS, FINELY
    CHOPPED (RESERVING SOME
    TO GARNISH)
60 G (½ CUP) CAPERBERRIES,
    SLICED
3 TABLESPOONS MINI CAPERS
3 HANDFULS WILD BABY ROCKET
3 HANDFULS BABY SPINACH LEAVES

DRESSING
80 ML (⅓ CUP) WHITE BALSAMIC
    VINEGAR
80 ML (⅓ CUP) EXTRA-VIRGIN
    OLIVE OIL
2 TABLESPOONS HOMEMADE OR
    BEST-QUALITY WHOLE EGG
    MAYONNAISE
2 TABLESPOONS FRESH LEMON
    JUICE

Preheat the oven to 180°C. Line a large baking tray.

Cut the potatoes into halves or quarters, leaving the skin on. Place in a plastic bag with the olive oil and salt and shake to coat. Tip the potatoes out onto the prepared tray and roast for 1 hour, or until the potatoes are golden and crisp. Allow to cool to room temperature.

In a small bowl, whisk together the dressing ingredients and season to taste with sea salt and freshly ground black pepper. In a large bowl, toss together the potatoes, spring onions, caperberries, capers and dressing.

Just before serving, spread the rocket and spinach leaves on a large platter. Place the potato mixture on top of the leaves and only slightly mix. Garnish with the reserved spring onions.

Serves 12

Evy Royal

I was a young Israeli girl backpacking through Australia when I met and fell in love with Tony. We married and I stayed, making Sydney our home.

I have grown to love unusual and different recipes, especially those not found in stores or restaurants. This was probably inspired by my Moroccan grandmother and great-grandmother, who both used to make the most amazing dishes, basically Middle Eastern but often with an exciting Spanish slant. I am always trying to replicate those delicious tastes and beautiful smells of my childhood.

How could I not be inspired by my great-grandmother in Israel? She didn't make just one dessert for Shabbat, she made ten! She would bring them to our house in mysterious boxes and we would open each one with great anticipation, marvelling at each. We'd arrange them beautifully on a huge platter and then the family sat and ate and ate (and ate!) until we could eat no more. At that time I was young and not really interested in cooking, so I never asked for the recipes. Now I wish I had.

My mother shared with me her recipe for mamoul *many years ago. I started to make them, hesitantly at first and then practising and perfecting them over time. They are now absolutely my most favourite sweet treats to bake, reminding me of my rich and wonderful Middle Eastern heritage.*

MAMOUL

DOUGH
375 G (2½ CUPS) PLAIN FLOUR
200 G UNSALTED BUTTER, AT ROOM
    TEMPERATURE
3 TABLESPOONS ROSEWATER
    OR ORANGE BLOSSOM WATER (OR
    SUBSTITUTE MINERAL WATER)

STUFFING
2 TEASPOONS GROUND CINNAMON
2 TEASPOONS ICING SUGAR
12 DATES, PITTED BUT LEFT WHOLE
50 G (½ CUP) PECANS OR WALNUTS
1 TABLESPOON PINE NUTS
EXTRA ICING SUGAR, FOR DUSTING

Preheat the oven to 180°C. Line a baking tray.

To make the dough, mix the flour, butter and rosewater together by hand and knead lightly to form a soft dough.

To make the stuffing, first mix the cinnamon and icing sugar together. Through the opening of each date, sprinkle a little of the cinnamon sugar inside. Stuff with one or two nuts, a couple of pine nuts and some more cinnamon sugar. Close the date, cut into three pieces and roll each piece in cinnamon sugar.

Take a small piece of dough (about a tablespoonful) and roll into a pliable ball. Flatten into a disc and then shape it into a little cup. Put the date piece inside, close the dough over the date and reshape into a smooth ball, removing as much excess dough as you can. Place on the prepared tray and prick with a fork. Repeat with all the dough and filling. Bake for 20 minutes, being careful that the biscuits don't brown. When cool, dust with icing sugar.

Makes about 36

Hamantashen are a traditional triangular biscuit made on the festival of Purim. When my kids were young, they would bring home hamantashen from kindy. I thought that I could definitely improve on the recipe, so I searched for the best recipe and then made a version using my own special filling.

HAMANTASHEN

DOUGH
450 G (3 CUPS) PLAIN FLOUR
½ TEASPOON BAKING POWDER
½ TEASPOON FINELY GRATED
    LEMON ZEST
200 G UNSALTED BUTTER, AT ROOM
    TEMPERATURE
4 EGG YOLKS
½ TEASPOON VANILLA EXTRACT
115 G (½ CUP) SUGAR
150 G SOUR CREAM

HALVA AND CHOCOLATE FILLING
250 G BEST-QUALITY HALVA,
    CUT ROUGHLY INTO 1 CM CUBES
150 G BEST-QUALITY COOKING
    CHOCOLATE, CUT INTO PIECES
    HALF THE SIZE OF THE HALVA
    CUBES

To make the dough, combine all the dough ingredients either in a food processor or by hand. Form the dough into a ball, wrap in plastic wrap and rest in the fridge for 1 hour.

Preheat the oven to 180°C. Line a baking tray.

Roll the dough out to a 3 mm thickness. Using a cookie cutter or small glass (8–9 cm in diameter), cut out circles from the dough. Place a cube of halva and a cube of chocolate on each circle. Bring three sides of the circle up into the centre, leaving a small opening at the top, to form a triangular pastry. Pinch the three joined edges to seal. Place on the prepared tray and bake for 20 minutes until golden.

Makes about 40

Note: There are many filling choices for the hamantashen. You can use jam, povidl (Hungarian plum jam) or nutella. You can also make a poppyseed or walnut filling, such as in Elisabeth Varnai's beigli (page 251).

Anat Shechter

For many generations, my family table has been a mouth-watering fusion of Ashkenazi and Sephardi cooking. In the late 1800s, my great-great-grandfather, Dr Menachem Stein, emigrated from Russia to Israel with his wife, Charlotte. I am so proud of the integral role he played in establishing modern Israel, founding the first Jewish hospital in Jaffa and the first neighbourhood of Tel Aviv. Charlotte used her talent for languages (seven of them) to promote culture, and shared recipes with her Arabic neighbours. Her passion for food flowed through to my grandparents who, in the 1940s, owned the well-known Blue Bird restaurant in Petach Tikva. Not only did they serve chicken soup to British soldiers, they also hid weapons for the underground movement under the floorboards!

Later they owned a food business specialising in movie catering, feeding stars such as Paul Newman and Kirk Douglas, while Simon and Garfunkel requested my grandmother's soup to recover from head colds. I loved schlepping with my grandparents on the catering bus over the summer holidays, watching my grandma Menachama hovering over the stoves. It was hot, there was no air-conditioner, so we were shvitzing constantly, but boy we were happy.

In the 1970s the different immigrant communities in Israel didn't share their cuisines, but today Israel is such a wonderful melting pot you would be lucky to find a meal that is purely from one culture or another.

I now live with my two children in Sydney, but my attitude to life is the same as always. Eat like there is no tomorrow!

To Israelis, hummus is like butter; we eat it with everything, on everything and all the time. I serve this hummus by spreading it onto a flat plate, drizzling olive oil around the perimeter and sprinkling it with paprika.

HUMMUS

400 G TIN ORGANIC CHICKPEAS, RINSED WELL AND DRAINED
185 ML (¾ CUP) WATER
2 CLOVES GARLIC
270 G (1 CUP) TAHINA PASTE
1 TEASPOON SALT, OR TO TASTE
¼ TEASPOON FRESHLY GROUND BLACK PEPPER
JUICE OF 1 LEMON

Using a food processor, blend the chickpeas and water for 2 minutes. Add the remaining ingredients and continue to process for at least 2 minutes until you have a smooth paste. Refrigerate for at least 1 hour, to thicken.

Makes 3 cups

This can be a dip, a spread or a salad dressing. And there is another secret — you can also cook with it. Cover your chicken, lamb or fish in lots of green tahini and bake it in the oven. You need real tahina paste (100 per cent sesame paste) for this recipe, not the ready-made tahini dip.

ABA ARYE'S (MY DAD'S) GREEN TAHINI

270 G (1 CUP) TAHINA PASTE
250 ML (1 CUP) WATER
170 ML (⅔ CUP) LEMON JUICE
2 TEASPOONS SALT
¼ TEASPOON FRESHLY GROUND
   BLACK PEPPER, OR TO TASTE
1 BUNCH PARSLEY, LEAVES ONLY
½ BUNCH CORIANDER, LEAVES
   ONLY
3 CLOVES GARLIC

Place all the ingredients in a food processor and blend for a few minutes until very well mixed.

Makes 3 cups

Matbucha is a very spicy Moroccan dip or condiment, with an Israeli twist. We love to have it in our pita with hummus or in an omelette.

MATBUCHA

2 LARGE GREEN CHILLIES, CHOPPED
2 LARGE RED CHILLIES, CHOPPED
800 G TIN DICED TOMATOES
185 ML (¾ CUP) VEGETABLE OIL
2–3 TEASPOONS SALT, OR TO TASTE
FRESHLY GROUND BLACK PEPPER,
   TO TASTE
13 CLOVES GARLIC, SLICED
1 TEASPOON SUGAR
1 HEAPED TABLESPOON SWEET
   PAPRIKA

Place all the ingredients in a saucepan or frying pan and bring to the boil. Reduce the heat to very low and simmer for 1 hour, stirring occasionally, until the liquid has reduced and the mixture has thickened.

Makes 2 cups

This Moroccan dish has now made its way to most Ashkenazi Shabbat tables in Israel. It is not to be confused with haraymeh, the Tunisian version of Friday night fish. There is a real rivalry between these two dishes — you can't like both. Serve this as part of a starter, spread with hummus, green tahina and matbucha. Alternatively, serve as a main course with rice or couscous.

MOROCCAN FISH

13 LARGE CHILLIES, HALVED
   LENGTHWAYS AND SEEDED
25 CLOVES GARLIC, PEELED AND
   LEFT WHOLE
1 BUNCH CORIANDER, LEAVES AND
   STEMS, ROUGHLY CHOPPED
800 G SKINLESS THICK WHITE FISH
   FILLETS, SUCH AS LING, BLUE
   EYE TREVALLA OR BARRAMUNDI,
   CUT INTO 8 PIECES
3 TABLESPOONS SWEET PAPRIKA
125 ML (½ CUP) VEGETABLE OIL
1 TEASPOON SALT
CHOPPED CORIANDER LEAVES,
   TO SERVE

Layer the chillies, whole cloves of garlic and half the coriander in the base of a large, deep frying pan. Place the fish pieces on top. Generously sprinkle with half the paprika and some of the oil, then turn the fish over and repeat. Top with the remaining coriander and oil. Sprinkle with the salt.

Cover the frying pan and bring to a simmer on a medium heat for 5–10 minutes, or until the fish is cooked. After 5 or so minutes, check the fish. There should be a small amount of liquid in the bottom of the pan. Season to taste. Leave to cool to room temperature for several hours. Sprinkle with coriander to serve.

Serves 8 as a starter

Every Middle Eastern country claims fame to this delicious, easy rice dish. My familiarity with majadara scored me lots of brownie points as a soldier guarding the borders between Jordan and Israel. In order to break the tension between us and the Palestinian women crossing the border, I used to ask them what was their secret to the perfect majadara; they were so happy with the question that it created a bridge between us. Food can build bridges to friendship; it is above all boundaries.

MAJADARA

200 G (1 CUP) BASMATI RICE
375 ML (1½ CUPS) WATER
60 ML (¼ CUP) VEGETABLE OIL
1 ONION, HALVED AND FINELY
　SLICED
2 TEASPOONS GROUND CUMIN
400 G TIN LENTILS, RINSED AND
　DRAINED

Put the rice and water in a saucepan and bring to the boil, then reduce the heat to low, cover and steam for 10 minutes until cooked. Alternatively, use a rice cooker.

Heat the oil in a frying pan and gently fry the onion until golden brown. Add the cumin and fry for 1 minute to release the aroma. Add the lentils to the pan and gently heat through. Add the lentil mixture to the cooked rice and combine well.

Serves 6–8 as a side dish

The Singers

Carole Singer

I grew up in Sydney with a Scottish Jewish mother, Millie, who was a consummate entertainer and talented baker. I remember there were always fresh batches of biscuits arranged in perfect rows on trays scattered around her tiny kitchen, their sweet vanilla or nutty aromas wafting all the way up the street. My mother hosted legendary afternoon teas, and made all her own pastries, including puff pastry cream horns, choux pastry cream puffs and éclairs, as well as scones, biscuits and cakes.

I married David and we had four children. Aside from the weekly Friday night dinner and lunch after shule on Saturday (with many visitors), our home was also the base where birthdays and festivals were celebrated. My kitchen was always on full power, churning out all the family and traditional favourites.

Debbi Weiss

Food and entertaining were always a central part of family life for me as a child. I think we all learnt how to say 'fress' before we learnt to say 'Mummy'! I have so many memories of lavish and plentiful tables and many people coming and going from our home.

My father's Polish mother, Tonia, was a traditional cook. Her secret to a happy husband, she claimed, was for 'him to smell fried onions as soon as he stepped into the house after a hard day's work.' She insisted we always call dishes by their Yiddish names, and was very intent on passing down traditional Jewish European cooking and eating habits. I remember her taking us to the movies once and handing out stuffed cabbage rolls for us to nibble on. Oh, the embarrassment. I would have given anything just for a choc top!

I became really interested in cooking when I was about twelve, and remember making my first croquembouche shaped around a Tupperware container, using my grandmother Millie's choux pastry recipe. She lived to 103 and I still use that recipe, as well as the others she taught me. When I got a kitchen of my own, Grandma Millie passed all her baking trays on to me, and I treasure them to this day.

I'm very intuitive with my cooking. I love playing with flavours, especially fresh herbs, to create new recipes. I have a 'happy cooking' philosophy — put on the music, have fun and get the creative juices going.

Carole

OK … so it's only roast beef, but this is no ordinary roast! Good cuts of kosher meat are expensive and sometimes hard to find — and expensive doesn't always mean tender. My roast beef fillet is one of our favourite Shabbat treats, with a tenderising process to produce a succulent, tasty fillet. It's also very delicious sliced and served cold.

CAROLE'S ROAST BEEF

2 KG PIECE BEEF SCOTCH FILLET
5 CLOVES GARLIC, HALVED
1 TEASPOON SALT
¼ TEASPOON FRESHLY GROUND
   BLACK PEPPER
2 TEASPOONS GARLIC POWDER
2 TEASPOONS MUSTARD POWDER
2 LARGE ONIONS, THICKLY SLICED
250 ML (1 CUP) VEGETABLE OIL

Start this recipe the day before, marinating the beef. Completely line a baking dish with a large piece of foil (enough to cover up and around the meat). Cut ten slits (2 cm deep) into the beef and push a half clove of garlic into each slit.

Combine the salt, pepper, garlic powder and mustard powder to make a spice mix. Rub the spice mix all over the beef and place into the prepared dish. Spread the onions on top of and around the beef. Wrap in the foil and refrigerate overnight.

On the day of serving, remove the dish from the fridge. Allow the beef to come to room temperature. Meanwhile, preheat the oven to 200°C. Open the foil (don't remove it) around the beef and pour over the oil. Cook the beef, uncovered, with the foil opened loosely, for 40 minutes. If the fillet is bigger, allow an extra 20 minutes per kilogram of meat. Rest the beef for 15 minutes before slicing and serving.

Serves 10

Debbi

Beetroot — very Ashkenazi, and chickpeas — very Sephardi. This salad is a concoction of mine dedicated to unity! This recipe is best made using dried chickpeas and fresh beetroot. However, if you are short of time you can substitute 4 x 400 g tinned chickpeas (you'll need 5 cups rinsed and drained chickpeas) and 850 g tinned baby beetroot.

BEETROOT AND CHICKPEA SALAD

440 G (2 CUPS) DRIED CHICKPEAS,
    SOAKED IN WATER OVERNIGHT
GOOD PINCH OF SALT
1 KG BEETROOT (BABY IF
    POSSIBLE), SCRUBBED
OLIVE OIL, FOR DRIZZLING
2 HANDFULS BABY SPINACH LEAVES
4 STALKS CELERY, DICED
1 SPANISH (RED) ONION, DICED
1 TELEGRAPH CUCUMBER, SEEDED
    AND DICED
2 TABLESPOONS CHOPPED MINT
2 TABLESPOONS CHOPPED PARSLEY
200 G GOAT OR SHEEP FETA
    CHEESE, CRUMBLED

DRESSING
JUICE OF 2 LEMONS
1 CLOVE GARLIC
4 MINT LEAVES
60 ML (¼ CUP) OLIVE OIL
1 TABLESPOON SUGAR
½ BEETROOT (OR 60 ML/¼ CUP
    BEETROOT JUICE FROM TIN,
    IF USING)

Preheat the oven to 200°C for the beetroot.

Cook the soaked and drained chickpeas in a large saucepan with plenty of water for about 40–60 minutes until just tender. Add the salt to the water just before they have finished cooking. Drain and set aside to cool. This step is not necessary if using tinned chickpeas.

While the chickpeas are cooking, season the beetroot with salt and pepper. Drizzle with a little olive oil and wrap as a package in foil. Place on a baking tray and cook for 1 hour. When cool enough to handle, and wearing gloves, peel off the skins (tiny beetroot may not need peeling) and cut into quarters.

To make the dressing, put all the ingredients into a small blender, add 200 g (1 cup) of the cooked chickpeas and combine well. Season with salt and freshly ground black pepper to taste.

To assemble the salad, layer the spinach, beetroot, remaining chickpeas, celery, onion and cucumber in a serving bowl. Pour the dressing over the salad and sprinkle with the chopped herbs and feta cheese.

Serves 14

Debbi

Although we don't host our Shabbat dinners every week, this dish makes a regular appearance on the table when family come to our home on Friday nights. I look forward to cooking this for many more years, and hopefully will enjoy it one day at my own children's Shabbat tables.

COUSCOUS ROAST CHICKEN

COUSCOUS STUFFING
125 G (⅔ CUP) COUSCOUS
6 SAFFRON THREADS
FINELY GRATED ZEST OF 1 LEMON
    OR ORANGE
LARGE PINCH OF GROUND
    CINNAMON
185 ML (¾ CUP) BOILING CHICKEN
    STOCK
80 G (½ CUP) DRY-ROASTED
    ALMONDS OR PISTACHIOS,
    COARSELY CHOPPED
12 DRIED APRICOTS OR DATES,
    SLICED
2 TABLESPOONS CHOPPED PARSLEY
2 TABLESPOONS CHOPPED MINT

2 LARGE CHICKENS
125 ML (½ CUP) OLIVE OIL

Preheat the oven to 200°C. Grease a large roasting tin or baking dish.

To make the couscous stuffing, put the couscous, saffron, zest and cinnamon in a heatproof bowl and pour over the boiling chicken stock. Cover and leave to soak. After a few minutes, fluff with a fork, then add all the other stuffing ingredients.

Wash the chickens inside and out and pat dry with paper towel. Stuff each chicken lightly (don't press the filling into the chicken too firmly) with the couscous mixture and place in the prepared tin, breast side up. Tie the drumsticks together with kitchen string or baking paper.

Brush the chickens with the olive oil and season generously with salt and pepper. Roast for 20 minutes, then turn the oven down to 180°C and cook for a further 60–70 minutes, or until the chickens are golden brown and cooked through (the juices will run clear when the thigh is pierced with a skewer). To serve, cut each chicken into four and place on a serving dish. Sprinkle the couscous stuffing around the chicken pieces.

Serves 8

Barbara Solomon

My mother grew up in a modern orthodox Czech home where her parents valued education above everything; even the girls were encouraged to study and discouraged from the kitchen. My grandmother believed that 'any idiot can cook', and that cooking was only a necessity, not a skill.

My mother did not have a love of food or cooking, but she had a repertoire of Central European Jewish comfort food, all beautifully executed. Everything was prepared with a minimum of fuss, nothing was ever weighed or measured, nor was a recipe book ever consulted.

Not surprisingly, I wasn't really interested in food until I met the Solomon family in the 1970s. Unlike my family, they frequently ate in restaurants and had large family gatherings with abundant food. However, it was a present from my husband, Bruce, that really got me started — The Don Dunstan Cookbook. I started to cook for friends, excited to try new things, and a whole new world opened up to me, thanks to a slightly quirky South Australian premier!

I learnt about cooking for a crowd when we began to have most Shabbat dinners at our place. This is what I relished the most. Still today, we sit around the table with our three children and the extended family, often inviting another family as well. For us, it makes traditional Jewish life more current and relevant, and it is still the most wonderful way to keep the family together. And my cooking? Now it's a real passion, and I'm not sure what my grandmother would have to say about that!

This soup exemplifies the type of food I like to feed my family. It is healthy and nourishing, full of goodness and is made with ingredients that I often have in my pantry or freezer. To me, barley and chicken are a winning combination. It's best made with homemade chicken soup or stock.

CHICKEN AND BARLEY SOUP

2 TABLESPOONS OLIVE OIL
2 ONIONS, CHOPPED
2 CARROTS, PEELED AND CHOPPED
2 STALKS CELERY, CHOPPED
2 GARLIC CLOVES, CRUSHED
400 G TIN DICED TOMATOES
2 LITRES (8 CUPS) CHICKEN STOCK
  (SEE RECIPE BELOW)
200 G PEARL BARLEY
350 G (2 CUPS) SHREDDED COOKED
  CHICKEN MEAT
2 TABLESPOONS CHOPPED PARSLEY

Heat the olive oil in a large saucepan and cook the onions, carrots and celery until soft. Add the garlic to the pan and cook for a further 1–2 minutes, then add the tomatoes and stock and bring to the boil.

Add the barley and reduce the heat to a simmer, then cook for about 50 minutes, or until the barley is tender. Add the chicken and parsley, and stir through to heat. Season well with salt and pepper to taste.

Serves 8

BARBARA'S HOMEMADE CHICKEN STOCK

1 CHICKEN (PREFERABLY A
  BOILER), CUT UP, PLUS 2 FRAMES
1 HANDFUL GIBLETS, CLEANED
2 CARROTS, ROUGHLY CHOPPED
2 PARSNIPS, ROUGHLY CHOPPED
2 ONIONS, ROUGHLY CHOPPED
2 STALKS CELERY, WITH THE
  LEAVES, ROUGHLY CHOPPED
½ BUNCH PARSLEY
1 TABLESPOON BLACK
  PEPPERCORNS
1 TEASPOON SALT, OR TO TASTE

Place the chicken pieces in a large 8–10 litre stockpot and cover with water. Bring to the boil and skim off the scum. Add the rest of the ingredients and simmer for 2 hours.

Allow the chicken to cool a little and then take the meat off the bones. Reserve the meat. Strain the stock and allow to cool overnight in the fridge. Skim off the fat before using.

Makes about 5 litres stock and about 700 g chicken meat

Years ago there was a restaurant in Kings Cross called Mesclun that made the most amazing biscuits. It closed down after a few years but a friend found their wonderful recipe and gave it to me. I have been making them ever since.

HONEY MACADAMIA NUT WAFERS

100 G UNSALTED BUTTER, AT ROOM
    TEMPERATURE
165 G (¾ CUP) CASTER SUGAR
90 G (¼ CUP) HONEY
75 G (½ CUP) PLAIN FLOUR
2 (80 G) EGG WHITES
120 G (¾ CUP) BEST-QUALITY
    DARK CHOCOLATE CHIPS
120 G (¾ CUP) UNSALTED RAW
    MACADAMIA NUTS, CHOPPED

Preheat the oven to 180°C. Line three baking trays (38 x 26 cm) with baking paper.

Put the butter, sugar, honey, flour and egg whites in a food processor and process until well combined and the mixture is smooth. Spread thinly over the prepared trays. Sprinkle with the chocolate and nuts. Bake for 18–20 minutes, or until lightly browned and cooked through. Cool on the trays, then break into pieces and store in an airtight container.

I adapted this dessert from a recipe I found in Fresh from the Farmers' Market *by Janet Fletcher, and I've been making it for many years now. It is light, not too sweet and just a little acidic, so it's the perfect finishing note to a big meal.*

BLOOD ORANGE COMPOTE

6–8 LARGE BLOOD OR NAVEL
    ORANGES (OR A MIXTURE OF
    BOTH)
165 G (¾ CUP) SUGAR
250 ML (1 CUP) DRY WHITE WINE
1 CINNAMON STICK
2–3 CLOVES
2 X 5 MM THICK SLICES PEELED
    FRESH GINGER, LIGHTLY
    SMASHED
250 ML (1 CUP) WATER

Remove 4 wide strips of peel from 1 orange, making sure there is no pith, and reserve. Cut a thin slice off the top and bottom of each orange. Using a small paring knife, slice off the peel and pith. Cut between the membranes to remove the segments, and place in a serving bowl. Alternatively, cut the peeled oranges crossways into 5 mm thick slices.

In a saucepan, combine the remaining ingredients plus the reserved strips of orange peel. Bring to the boil and simmer on a medium heat, stirring to dissolve the sugar, for 10–15 minutes, or until the liquid is reduced to 375 ml (1½ cups). Strain the hot syrup and pour it over the fruit, adding the cinnamon stick to the fruit. Leave to cool. Cover and refrigerate for several hours or overnight. Serve chilled, with the honey macadamia wafers if desired.

Serves 6–8

May Stein

For me, growing up in Baghdad was unique. During the fierce dry heat of the summer months we sought refuge during the day in a cellar and slept on the flat roof terrace at night, under the moonlight and stars. What a treat that was!

We kept a kosher home and Friday nights were very special to our family; nothing was more important than each of us being present to welcome in Shabbat. In preparation for the meal, the chicken dealer arrived with a selection of live birds, one of which my mother carefully chose and then personally took to the shochet (slaughterer) around the corner. She was very clever in that the polkas (legs), wings and giblets from the chicken provided the soup and base for the okra dish (an aphrodisiac for Shabbat!) that we enjoyed on Friday night. She then made tebit, stuffing the body of the chicken with rice and spices, and putting it on to cook all night on a low flame, along with a dozen or so eggs, so we could have a festive hot meal, served with almonds and sultanas, without doing any actual cooking on the day of rest.

Life for the Jews was often fraught with difficulty. In 1941, the uprising of Rashid Ali and the pogrom (the Farhud) created huge unrest and we were sent to Bombay for seven months until it settled down. Unexpectedly, we did enjoy that time as we got to know our many relatives — my father had ten siblings living in India, each with their own family.

In 1948, after the War of Liberation, my family was given the choice by the British to either give up our passports or leave the country immediately. We left immediately for London; I was sixteen. By 1952 most Jews had left Iraq as the situation for them had become intolerable, and a record 120 000 Iraqi Jews left for Israel in one massive undertaking. In 1956 I moved to Israel, but it was on a visit to Australia to see my sister that I met my husband, Fred. We have been blessed with two sons, two gorgeous daughters-in-law and four grandchildren. They all love to eat and I am only too happy to feed them.

I first tasted this kugelhopf over thirty years ago at my old friend Susie Klein's house. It is an extremely moist and delicious chocolate- and white-swirled butter cake, which originally came from her German mother. I quickly scribbled the recipe down on a piece of paper and have been making it ever since.

KUGELHOPF

125 G UNSALTED BUTTER

200 G DARK CHOCOLATE,
   ROUGHLY CHOPPED

6 EGGS, SEPARATED

460 G (2 CUPS) CASTER SUGAR

300 G SOUR CREAM

300 G (2 CUPS) SELF-RAISING
   FLOUR

Preheat the oven to 220°C. Grease a 26 cm kugelhopf tin or bundt tin.

Melt the butter and set aside. Melt the chocolate in a double boiler or in a heatproof bowl over a saucepan of simmering water and set aside.

Beat the egg yolks with 230 g (1 cup) of the sugar until creamy. Add the sour cream and then the melted butter. Slowly add the flour and beat until well combined. In a separate bowl, whisk the egg whites until frothy and then add the remaining sugar, beating until stiff peaks form. Add the egg whites to the yolk mixture and carefully fold together to combine.

Pour two-thirds of the combined mixture into the prepared tin. Combine the melted chocolate with the remaining one-third of the mixture, then add the chocolate mixture to the tin. Bake for 9 minutes, then reduce the oven to 170°C and bake for a further 50 minutes, or until the cake feels firm to the touch. Leave to cool in the tin before turning out onto a wire rack.

Serves 12

Gretta Anna Teplitzky

New Zealand-born Gretta Anna lived a life rich with family, had a wonderfully supportive husband, David, created beautiful food and wrote iconic cookbooks. She passed away in 2010.

It was the simple gift from David of a huge French cookbook that was to prove life-changing for Gretta Anna. She took it into a long bath and read it from cover to cover, amazed and inspired by the possibilities it suggested. Despite having limited experience with cooking while growing up, she decided then and there that she was going to teach French cooking. She started small, inviting twelve friends to her first class, managing to just keep one step ahead of them each week. To her amazement, they loved it!

As the popularity of her classes grew, so did her awareness of the need for some formal training. She undertook short courses at Le Cordon Bleu in London and Paris, and travelled to other parts of the world to observe the best three-star Michelin restaurants. Back at home, she incorporated the best of what she'd learnt into what she called, 'new recipes for busy housewives wanting to entertain their husband's work associates and their own families'.

David and Gretta Anna were a great team. After starting a cooking school in the city and running additional classes in the north, they built a fully equipped cooking school, the Gretta Anna School of Cooking, beneath their home in Wahroonga. For an amazing forty years she taught classes for up to sixty people and raised her family with enormous energy and stamina. Her gift to others was to help people cook with confidence and ease. She believed that cooking was the best way to nurture and enrich family life.

Gretta Anna won many awards for her books, The Gretta Anna Recipes (1978) and More Gretta Anna Recipes (1989). David arranged the publishing, telling her that he was her 'sternest critic and most loving encourager'. Gretta Anna was so thrilled and proud that her love of cooking had been passed down to each of her children.

Palacsinta is a Hungarian chocolate pancake dessert. This lovely and often-made recipe was published in Gretta Anna's first book. It was the all-time favourite of her children and their spouses and children, and she found the time to teach all the grandchildren to make it. She used to say, 'It doesn't matter if you are a poor shot and the pancakes don't fall on top of each other; however they fall, it all works up beautifully into a rich, irresistible pudding.'

PALACSINTA

250 G UNSALTED BUTTER,
   AT ROOM TEMPERATURE
120 G SUGAR
6 EGGS, SEPARATED
1 TEASPOON VANILLA EXTRACT
185 ML (¾ CUP) MILK
90 G PLAIN FLOUR
BUTTER, FOR COOKING
DRINKING CHOCOLATE, FOR
   SPRINKLING
400 ML PURE CREAM (35% FAT)

You will need a crepe pan and an ovenproof dish, just slightly bigger than the diameter of the crepes.

Beat together the butter, sugar and egg yolks until light and fluffy. Add the vanilla to the milk and, alternating with the flour, add to the butter mixture, mixing thoroughly until the batter is thick. Don't worry if the mixture looks curdled, just continue with the recipe. In a separate bowl, whisk the egg whites until stiff peaks form, then fold into the batter.

Heat the crepe pan on a medium heat. Butter it thoroughly using a piece of crumpled greaseproof paper dipped in butter. Place 2 tablespoons of the mixture in the pan, swirling the pan to help the mixture spread, and cook until the underside is golden. Check this by lifting up the pancake with a small spatula and peeping underneath. Lift the pancake out of the pan and turn it upside down into the ovenproof dish (the cooked side should be facing upwards). Sprinkle the top with 1½ tablespoons of the drinking chocolate. Continue making the pancakes until all the mixture is used, turning out each one on top of the previous, sprinkling chocolate between each. You should have a reasonably straight stack, but it does not need to be perfect.

Near serving time, preheat the oven to 180°C. Pour the cream over the pancake stack and cook for 30–35 minutes. Serve hot, with nothing but the chocolate sauce that forms around the pancake from the cream and chocolate.

Serves 8

Gretta Anna made this at least once a week for her 'custard–loving husband'. It's a really quick yet sophisticated dessert that can be made in record time, and then can wait in the fridge to be served. If you like, sprinkle the custard with flaked almonds and caster sugar instead of nutmeg.

BAKED CUSTARD WITH CRUSHED STRAWBERRIES

CUSTARD
600 ML PURE CREAM (35% FAT)
300 ML MILK
3 TABLESPOONS CASTER SUGAR
3 LARGE EGGS
DASH OF VANILLA EXTRACT
GROUND NUTMEG, FOR
   SPRINKLING

500 G (2 PUNNETS) STRAWBERRIES,
   HULLED AND WASHED
1½ TABLESPOONS ICING SUGAR
   MIXTURE
60 ML (¼ CUP) GRAND MARNIER,
   OR TO TASTE
WHIPPED CREAM, TO SERVE

Preheat the oven to 150°C. You will need a 1.5 litre (6 cup) ovenproof dish.

To make the custard, place all the custard ingredients (except the nutmeg) in a large bowl and beat well to dissolve the sugar. Pour into the prepared dish. Put the custard dish in a large, deep baking tin and pour in enough hot water to come halfway up the side of the custard dish. Sprinkle with nutmeg and bake for 1¼–1½ hours until the custard is set but still slightly wobbly. Remove from the oven. Cool, then remove from the water bath and place in the fridge to chill for several hours or overnight.

Finely slice the strawberries and sprinkle with the icing sugar, then crush with a potato masher. Add the liqueur, to taste, and mix well. Place in the fridge to chill. Serve the baked custard with the crushed strawberries and whipped cream.

Serves 8

The Varnais

Elisabeth Varnai

Sydney became my home in 1956 after escaping post-war Hungary with my husband, George, and our young son. My sisters and I, unlike our poor parents, miraculously survived the war, which for me was spent in a concentration camp from the age of sixteen. Once we settled in Australia, we began to enjoy life again. It was distant from the horrors we all experienced in Europe and we relished the opportunity to start afresh.

To us, family was everything. Our wonderful children, their partners, our three grandchildren and the extended family network of sisters and brothers-in-law, nieces and nephews, were all important. Many celebrations and feasts were shared and my sisters and I prepared countless dishes from our 'old country', and then enjoyed them together. This was the way we kept our heritage alive. With George now no longer with us, I am still very involved with my family, and even though I don't cook as much as I used to, I still love to cook for my grandchildren.

Kathy Goldberg

Even though I was born in Sydney, I still have a strong sense of my Hungarian heritage. My parents and brother spoke Hungarian at home so I am also fluent, and really enjoy being able to communicate with those who speak Hungarian better than they speak English. Just from standing next to my mother in the kitchen, watching and helping her, I learnt so many wonderful recipes. I still enjoy cooking Hungarian food because I love the flavours I grew up with and most dishes can be prepared in advance, which suits our busy lifestyle.

When our extended family gets together on a Friday night, it's a great opportunity to cook up a storm, catch up and overindulge — just a little! Over the years I have built up a selection of firm family favourites that the kids often ask for. These are my own food traditions for which, hopefully, I'll be remembered in the generations to follow.

Elisabeth

When I was growing up, my mother used to make beigli, *a type of strudel, for the family. Sadly, the recipe was lost. During my early days in Sydney I visited a friend for afternoon tea and was delighted to be served these* beigli, *and I've been making them ever since. This recipe makes six balls of dough. Any you don't need can be kept in the freezer for several months — handy when you want to quickly whip up a batch. Start this recipe the day before you need it.*

BEIGLI (POPPYSEED AND WALNUT)

DOUGH

1 KG (6⅔ CUPS) SELF-RAISING
   FLOUR
500 G (3⅓ CUPS) PLAIN FLOUR
PINCH OF SALT
25 G CASTER SUGAR
750 G UNSALTED BUTTER, AT ROOM
   TEMPERATURE
6 EGG YOLKS
450 G SOUR CREAM
ABOUT 250 ML (1 CUP) SODA
   WATER

1½ TABLESPOONS APRICOT JAM
2 EGG YOLKS, BEATEN, FOR
   GLAZING
VANILLA ICING SUGAR (SEE
   NOTE, PAGE 149), FOR SERVING
   (OPTIONAL)

To make the dough, mix together the flours, salt and sugar in a bowl. Rub the butter in with your fingertips until it is spread throughout the flour. Mix in the egg yolks, then add the sour cream. Mix with your hands, gradually adding enough of the soda water until you have a smooth dough that is not sticky and there is no flour left in the bottom of the bowl.

Divide the dough into six balls, each about 500 g. On a floured board, knead each ball for a few minutes with the heel of your hand, kneading back and forth along the board until the dough is a smooth, silky ball. Wrap each ball in plastic wrap and freeze for at least 24 hours. Defrost at room temperature to use.

Preheat the oven to 180°C. On a floured board, roll out a ball of dough to a 2 mm thickness, to form a 40 x 30 cm rectangle or oval shape. Spread a thin layer of apricot jam over the dough from edge to edge, then spread with the walnut or poppyseed filling. Loosely roll up the dough from the long edge to form a long round log. Do not flatten it. Brush with the egg glaze and pierce with two rows of fork pricks along the top. Place on a lined baking tray and bake for 40 minutes, or until golden on top. Allow to cool, then slice on the diagonal into 1.5–2 cm wide slices. Sprinkle with vanilla icing sugar to serve if you wish.

The dough makes 6 balls; each ball makes 1 beigli roll, or 20–25 pieces

POPPYSEED FILLING (FOR ONE ROLL)

200 G POPPYSEEDS, FRESHLY
 GROUND
165 G (¾ CUP) SUGAR, OR TO
 TASTE
25 G (1 SACHET) VANILLA SUGAR
 (SEE NOTE, PAGE 150)
1 SMALL HANDFUL (40 G)
 SULTANAS
375 ML (1½ CUPS) MILK
2 EGG WHITES

To make the poppyseed filling, place all the ingredients, except the egg whites, in a saucepan. Cook on a medium heat for about 15 minutes, stirring frequently, until it has reduced to become a fairly solid, but still moist, mixture. Allow to cool. Lightly beat the egg whites together until white and frothy, but not stiff. Mix the egg whites through the poppyseed mixture.

WALNUT FILLING (FOR ONE ROLL)

250 G WALNUTS, GROUND
220 G (1 CUP) SUGAR
1 SMALL HANDFUL (40 G)
 SULTANAS
FINELY GRATED ZEST OF ½ LEMON
1½ TEASPOONS TEA RUM
 (OR OTHER RUM)
2 EGG WHITES

To make the walnut filling, mix together all the ingredients, except the egg whites, in a bowl. Lightly beat the egg whites until white and frothy, but not stiff. Mix the egg whites through the walnut mixture.

Elisabeth

Chicken paprikash is probably one of the best-known Hungarian dishes, and everyone I know makes their own version of it. This is mine, and I have been feeding my family this for over fifty years! I like to serve them with nokedli, small pea-sized dumplings, which perfectly soak up the sauce from the chicken.

CHICKEN PAPRIKASH

1 TABLESPOON VEGETABLE OIL
1 ONION, CHOPPED
2 TEASPOONS HUNGARIAN RED
   PAPRIKA (SWEET)
1 CHICKEN, CUT INTO 4 OR
   8 PIECES
¼ GREEN CAPSICUM, ROUGHLY
   CHOPPED
1 SMALL TOMATO, ROUGHLY
   CHOPPED
2 TEASPOONS PLAIN FLOUR
125 ML (½ CUP) WATER OR
   CHICKEN STOCK

Heat the oil in a deep frying pan and cook the onion until well browned. Add the paprika and cook for 2 minutes, then add the chicken pieces and brown well. Add the capsicum and tomato and cook, covered, for 25–30 minutes, or until the chicken is almost cooked through. Remove the chicken from the pan.

Sprinkle the flour over the sauce in the pan and stir through until bubbling. Push the sauce and vegetables through a sieve, then return the strained sauce to the pan. Discard the remnants. Add the water or stock to the sauce and cook, stirring, for a few minutes until thickened. Return the chicken to the pan and cook, uncovered, for 10 minutes, basting occasionally, until cooked through. Reheat and serve with nokedli.

Serves 4

NOKEDLI

500 G (3⅓ CUPS) PLAIN FLOUR
1½ TEASPOONS SALT
3 EGGS
375 ML (1½ CUPS) WATER
VEGETABLE OIL, TO SERVE

Put the flour and salt in a bowl and make a well in the centre. Add the eggs to the well and beat with a fork. Slowly incorporate the flour, adding a little water at a time until you have a thick batter, with the consistency of porridge. Use a whisk or wooden spoon to beat until smooth. Add a little water if it is too thick.

Bring a large saucepan of salted water to the boil. Using a sieve with large holes or a nokedli or spaetzle maker, push the batter through the holes, letting small pieces fall into the water. If using a sieve, use a spatula to press the mixture through the holes. The nokedli will rise to the surface after a couple of minutes. Cook for a further 5–8 minutes, or until you taste they are cooked. Drain and toss with a little oil to serve. Refresh in cold water if serving later.

Kathy

My late mother-in-law taught me to make this cake when I married her son, telling me that delicious food was definitely the way to his heart and this was one of his favourites. It has now become part of what I like to cook and is a happy reminder of her. Her secret with the paper and pins really works.

BUCHE DE CHOCOLAT

225 G BEST-QUALITY DARK
    CHOCOLATE, CHOPPED
1 TEASPOON INSTANT COFFEE
    DISSOLVED IN 80 ML (⅓ CUP)
    HOT WATER
7 EGGS, SEPARATED
230 G (1 CUP) CASTER SUGAR
300 ML PURE CREAM (35% FAT)
2 TEASPOONS ICING SUGAR
1 VANILLA BEAN, SEEDS SCRAPED
2 TABLESPOONS COCOA POWDER

RASPBERRY COULIS
500 G FRESH OR FROZEN
    RASPBERRIES
40 G (¼ CUP) ICING SUGAR,
    OR TO TASTE

Preheat the oven to 170°C. Line the base of a 38 x 26 cm swiss roll tin with baking paper. You will need a few dressmaking pins to secure the cake.

Melt the chocolate with the coffee and water in a double boiler or in a heatproof bowl over a saucepan of simmering water. Allow to cool slightly. Beat the egg whites until stiff peaks form. In a separate bowl, beat the egg yolks with the sugar until pale and fluffy, then beat in the melted chocolate. Fold this mixture into the egg whites and spread it out into the prepared tin. Bake for 20 minutes, or until a skewer inserted into the cake comes out clean. When the cake is cool, cover with a tea towel and put in the fridge for 1 hour.

Beat the cream with the icing sugar and vanilla seeds until thick, and set aside. Sift the cocoa powder over the cake, then cover with a piece of baking paper and turn it over. Remove the tin and the baking paper that was on the base of the cake.

Place the cream in the middle third of the cake, along its full length, and make a large long log as follows. Lift up the two long sides of the cake and bring them over to meet in the middle, sliding one side under the other to encase the cream. Using dressmaking pins to secure the package, join the paper and fold down, holding the paper tightly around the log to help hold its shape. Put the cake in the fridge until ready to serve.

To make the raspberry coulis, put the raspberries and icing sugar into a blender and purée. Sieve to remove the seeds. Remove the paper from the cake and serve with the coulis and extra raspberries or mixed berries.

Serves 8–10

Judy Wilkenfeld

My love of food grew from spending many weekends with my maternal grandmother, watching her cook. I can still taste the wonderful cinnamon and sugar biscuits she made, which we used to dunk into a hot cup of tea, and I remember how fascinating it was to watch her make lokshen, the noodles for chicken soup. My parents worked full-time, and after school my mother would phone with instructions on how to prepare dinner with what she had defrosted earlier. After a while I started experimenting with whatever was in the cupboard, adding a bit of this or that to her dishes to enhance the flavours.

For a while I lived in Israel where I learnt to prepare the 'old world' and traditional Eastern European Jewish foods. Bob Cadry, my ex-husband, and his family, originally from Persia, were my introduction to the exotic Persian-style of cooking. Friday nights involved at least twenty around the table. My mother-in-law would come into my kitchen, lift the lid on each pot and ask, 'What's this?' She seemed content that I, her Australian/European daughter-in-law, could cook these dishes almost as well as she could!

However, it was our upstairs neighbour, a lovely Persian lady, Angie, who really taught me the finer aspects of Persian cooking. We could smell each other's cooking wafting up and down the stairwell and would get together in one or the other's kitchen, comparing notes, then finally sharing a wonderful meal. I still love cooking this food, particularly for my three children, who all love good food and are excellent cooks, too. In fact, Angie now teaches my daughter, Lainie! And so, the tradition continues …

Kukuye sabsi *is a Persain-style omelette, similar to a frittata, and is often served on New Year's Day in Iran. The secret of the texture is to chop the parsley coarsely, not finely.*

KUKUYE SABSI

6 EGGS
1 BUNCH FLAT-LEAF PARSLEY, LEAVES COARSELY CHOPPED, STEMS DISCARDED
3 SPRING ONIONS, FINELY CHOPPED
¾ TEASPOON CRUSHED GARLIC
1 TABLESPOON OLIVE OIL
RADISHES, MINT AND/OR SPRING ONIONS, TO GARNISH
YOGHURT, TO SERVE

Lightly whisk the eggs together. Add the parsley, spring onions and garlic. Season with salt and pepper and combine well.

Heat the olive oil in a non-stick frying pan on a low–medium heat until hot. Add the egg mixture and cook for 5 minutes. Turn the omelette carefully onto a plate and then slide it back into the pan and cook the other side for 5 minutes, or until set. Slice into wedges and serve either warm or cold, with the garnishes and a dollop of yoghurt.

Serves 2–4

This dish is reminiscent of many of the stews that I learnt to make years ago. I always travelled far and wide to source the herbs and spices needed, and I recall fondly how in the early days Bob and I would return from holidays in Los Angeles with our bags stuffed with all the 'special ingredients' we had found, which weren't available in Sydney at that time.

PERSIAN QUINCE STEW (KHORESH-E BEH)

80 ML (⅓ CUP) VEGETABLE OIL

2 ONIONS, FINELY SLICED

2 KG VEAL GOULASH (STEWING VEAL SUCH AS BONELESS VEAL SHOULDER)

½ TEASPOON GROUND CINNAMON

2 LARGE QUINCES, WASHED WELL

3 TABLESPOONS SUGAR

3 HEAPED TABLESPOONS TOMATO PASTE

JUICE OF 1 LEMON

2 TABLESPOONS QUINCE PASTE, OR USE APRICOT JAM FOR A SWEETER TASTE

Heat 3 tablespoons of the oil in a large pot and cook the onions until golden brown. Add the meat and brown lightly, then add the cinnamon and season with salt and pepper. Add enough water so the meat is just covered, then cover with a lid and simmer over a low heat for 1 hour, stirring occasionally.

Meanwhile, halve, core and seed (use an apple corer) the quinces but do not peel them. Slice as for thick apple pie pieces. Heat the remaining oil in a frying pan on a medium heat and brown the quinces in batches until deep golden. Set aside.

When the meat is ready, add the quinces, sugar, tomato paste, lemon juice and quince paste to the pot. Cover and simmer for a further 1 hour, or until the meat and fruit are tender. When stirring, try not to break the quinces' crescent shape. Taste and adjust the seasoning; the flavour should be both sweet and sour. Serve with gobehli rice (page 260) or couscous.

Serves 8

Rice is the most important part of the meal in the Persian culture. The source and quality of the rice was essential. I would drive 90 minutes to get the perfect sack of rice if my parents-in-law were coming to dinner. As they sat down to eat, the rice was examined from every aspect. The grains had to be really long from being washed well and had to have the right colour, the cooked rice had to be salted perfectly, it had to be just fluffy and not too gluggy, and the crispness on the outside had to be perfectly executed. This crunchy rice crust is known in Persian as the thadig, *and it's often the best part!*

WHITE GOBEHLI RICE

800 G (4 CUPS) LONG-GRAIN
   BASMATI RICE
ABOUT 1.375 LITRES (5½ CUPS)
   WATER
1 TEASPOON SALT
VEGETABLE OIL

Rinse the rice in a pot of cold water seven to ten times, or until the water runs clear and the rice grains have changed from translucent to an almost solid white. Use a gentle circular motion to wash the rice so you agitate the starch out of it. Drain the rice and put it in a non-stick rice cooker. Make sure the rice is level, then touch the top of the rice with the tip of your index finger. Pour in as much of the water as necessary to come up to the first crease on your finger. Season with the salt. Cook the rice following the cooking times recommended for your brand of rice cooker. Leave the cooked rice on the warm setting.

If you don't have a rice cooker, bring the water and rice to the boil in a large heavy-based non-stick saucepan. Cover and turn the heat down to low. Steam the rice for about 20–30 minutes, or until cooked. Turn the heat off until ready to toast the rice.

Ten minutes before you are ready to serve, remove the inner pan from the rice cooker (or use the saucepan it was cooked in). Using a flat spatula, create a cone shape from the outside of the pan towards the centre – like a mountain peak. Pour a small amount of oil around the edge of the pan and a little dash in the middle. Place a tea towel over the pan and put a lid over the cloth. Turn the stove on to a low heat and place the pan with the cooked rice in it directly on the stove. After at least 10 minutes, or when you hear a crackling sound, take the pan off the heat. Using your rice paddle, loosen the rice slightly around the sides, checking if the rice has browned underneath. Flip the pan upside down onto a large flat plate. The rice should have formed a delicious crusty golden layer, which will now be sitting on the top.

Serves 10–12

Chanie Wolff

I always say (jokingly of course) that one of the reasons I agreed to marry my husband was so I could join the Wolff family and get his mother Sonia's much talked about challah recipe. I was definitely not disappointed! My family know that they are in for a Shabbat treat when I bake 'Bubby's special challah'. This amazing, tried, tested and much loved recipe has been kindly passed on from her, a recipe that has been in their family for many many years.

It is also delicious when baked as onion challah. Sonia once chanced upon this variation by accident when rushed for time. Instead of baking it as a traditional challah, she threw raw diced onions, oil and coarse salt over the dough and baked it as usual. It was a delightful result.

My husband, Levi Wolff, serves as the Rabbi at a wonderful congregation, The Central Synagogue, in Bondi Junction. Levi now belongs to the fourth generation of his family who have committed their lives to spreading the warmth and beauty of Judaism across the globe. Moving from the USA via Perth, Sydney is now home to us and our six children.

We love inviting members of our congregation to Shabbat lunch at our home, when I prepare a typical meal including chopped liver, challah and cholent. It makes me proud to think that this beautiful challah recipe has been enjoyed by tens of thousands of Jewish men and women who have graced the many Shabbat tables of the Wolff family and their ancestors across the world.

Baking your own challah on a Friday is a special mitzvah (spiritual good deed) for Jewish women. I double the recipe and, before plaiting, remove a small piece of the dough and say the blessing, 'Baruch ata adonai, elohaynu melech ha'olam asher kideshanu bemitzvotav vetzivanu al afrashat chala.' This is symbolic of the days of the temple and brings blessing to the home and family.

CHALLAH FROM HEAVEN

1 KG (6⅔ CUPS) PLAIN FLOUR,
 PLUS 75 G (½ CUP) EXTRA
560 ML (2¼ CUPS) WARM WATER
18 G (2½ SACHETS) DRIED YEAST
170 G (¾ CUP) CASTER SUGAR
1½ HEAPED TABLESPOONS SALT
2 EGGS, BEATEN
125 ML (½ CUP) VEGETABLE OIL
1 EGG, BEATEN, FOR GLAZING
POPPYSEEDS OR SESAME SEEDS

Put 500 g of the flour in a large bowl. Make a large well in the flour and add the warm water. Add the yeast and 115 g (½ cup) of the sugar, stirring the yeast and water in the well until combined. Set aside for 15 minutes, or until the yeast is foamy.

Add the salt and remaining sugar to the well and mix. Wait another 5–10 minutes for the mixture to foam again, then add the eggs and oil and mix with a wooden spoon. Gradually incorporate the flour in the bowl into the egg mixture in the well. Once combined, add enough of the remaining 500 g of flour to form a dough, tip it onto a floured surface, and knead in the remainder. If the dough is too sticky, slowly add the extra flour. Knead for 10 minutes until you have a smooth, slightly sticky dough.

Place in a large oiled bowl and cover with a tea towel. Set aside in a warm place and allow the dough to rise until it has doubled in bulk (this will take 2–3 hours). When the dough has risen, divide it into two equal pieces. Shape each piece into a plaited loaf (see note).

Preheat the oven to 180°C. Place the loaves on a lightly greased baking tray and allow them to rise for at least 30 minutes and up to 1 hour. Brush with the egg wash and sprinkle with the seeds. Bake for 45 minutes, or until golden in colour. Remove from the tray and allow to cool.

Makes 2 medium challahs

Note: The simplest way to plait a challah is to divide the dough into three long sausages. Pinch them together at the end and plait as you would plait hair. Pinch together the other end to join and tuck under slightly. For a more decorative challah, make a four- or six-strand plait.

GLOSSARY

Ashkenazi Jews of Eastern European descent.

babke A type of Eastern European cake, usually made with yeast.

balabusta Yiddish term meaning 'excellent homemaker'; quite an accolade. The word comes from the Hebrew for 'head of the household'.

Bar Mitzvah The 'coming of age' of a Jewish boy (at age 13) when he reads special passages from the Bible (Torah) and his family and friends celebrate with him.

beschert Yiddish word meaning 'meant to be', almost 'preordained'.

bissel Yiddish word meaning 'just a little bit' – a *bissel* sugar in my tea, a *bissel* cream on my cake.

blintzes Thin crepes with savoury (often meat) or sweet (often cheese) fillings, which are then folded or rolled into parcels; of Eastern European origin.

Bobba/Booby/Buba/Bubba A term of endearment used for a grandmother.

challah (pronounced HAH-lah) A traditional Jewish plaited yeast bread (often enriched with egg) prepared for festivals and Shabbat; served in pairs.

charoset A delicious combination of apple, walnuts, cinnamon and wine eaten at the Passover feast to represent the mortar (cement) used by the Jewish people when they were slaves in Egypt. Excellent on top of matzo.

cholent A traditional Jewish dish of (usually) meat, potatoes, beans and barley, which is made before Shabbat begins on a Friday, then slowly cooks all night and is served for lunch on Saturday.

fress Yiddish word meaning 'to eat with gusto', as the Jewish people do very well.

gefilte fish A traditional Jewish dish of minced and well-seasoned fish, which is then made into patties and boiled in stock. Traditionally served with a slice of carrot on top and horseradish on the side.

hamantashen A sweet three-cornered filled pastry served at Purim, representing the ears of Haman, the villain of this festival.

kneidlach Also known as matzo balls, these traditional Jewish dumplings (made from matzo meal, eggs and schmaltz) are served in chicken soup at the Passover feast. Every cook believes theirs are the best and they have therefore not been included in this book.

kosher If you keep kosher, you follow the Jewish dietary laws; for example, not eating meat and milk products at the same meal, and not eating shellfish, pig products and certain other fish and animals.

labna A thick yoghurt cheese, which can be store bought or made at home by draining yoghurt (mixed with a little salt) over muslin in the fridge for a couple of days.

latkes Crisp fried potato pancakes eaten in abundance during the Festival of Lights (Chanukah) to commemorate the miracle when the eternal flame in the Jerusalem temple lasted on one day's oil for a full eight days.

lokshen Egg noodles, homemade or store bought, eaten in chicken soup or mixed with eggs and other ingredients to make a sweet or savoury pudding (*kugel*).

lox Another name for sliced smoked salmon, particularly associated with bagels, cream cheese and Sunday brunch.

matzo/matzo meal An unleavened bread, like a large square water cracker, eaten at Passover. Matzo meal is ground matzo and is available in coarse, fine or superfine varieties.

mitzvah Strictly means one of the 613 commandments from the Bible (Torah), but has also come to mean a good deed or act of kindness.

Palmach The elite fighting force of the Jewish army during the British Mandate of Palestine from 1941–1948.

Passover (Pesach) An eight-day festival celebrating the Jewish people being freed from slavery in Egypt. During this time, bread is not eaten so as to remember when the Jews had to leave Egypt in such a hurry that there was no time for their bread to rise; therefore, matzo is eaten instead. Passover is a time to feast on biscuits and cakes, all specially baked without flour or rising agents.

perogen Little pastry or dough dumplings of Eastern European origin, traditionally filled with meat, cheese or potato.

pischinger An Austro-Hungarian cake of wafer layers and cocoa cream.

povidl Hungarian plum jam or conserve, available in gourmet stores.

Purim The festival celebrating the time when the Jews in ancient Persia were saved from being the victims of an evil decree against them. It is traditional to eat *hamantashen* filled with jam, poppyseeds or chocolate, and prepare food baskets for the poor.

Rosh Hashanah The Jewish New Year, celebrated with prayers and much feasting, particularly apples dipped in honey (for a sweet year) and honey cake.

schmaltz The direct translation is 'fat'. In cooking, it is the rendered fat of a chicken; on your body, it is the result of too much schmaltz in your cooking.

Sephardi In essence, Jews of Iberian Peninsula (now Spain and Portugal) descent, but nowadays it has a wider meaning and includes Jews who are not Ashkenazi, for example of Iraqi, Indian and North African origin.

Shabbat The Sabbath, a day of complete rest. Begins at sunset on Friday and ends at sunset on Saturday; no work, much prayer and abundant eating.

shtetl Typically a small Eastern European town (19th century to mid-20th century) with a large Jewish population, but now can also refer to a close-knit community.

shule Synagogue, the Jewish house of prayer.

shvitzing Sweating, either literally or figuratively.

simcha A celebration of any type, most often referring to a wedding or Bar/Bat Mitzvah.

sweet sacramental wine Also known as Kiddush wine, a sweet red wine used to make a blessing on wine. In recipes, port can be substituted.

Yiddish The old spoken language of many Ashkenazi Jews; a mix between German, Hebrew and other languages. Now it is mainly used by parents who don't want their children to understand what they are saying, and for those words that have no direct translation in English.

Yiddishkeit Literally means 'Jewishness' but has come to mean a feeling of actively participating in Jewish tradition and culture.

Yom Kippur The Day of Atonement, when the Jewish people atone for their sins. It is a solemn day of fasting, which ends with the blowing of the Shofar (a ram's horn) and yet another feast.

INDEX

INTERNATIONAL CONVERSIONS

DRY MEASURES

Metric	Imperial
15 G	½ OZ
30 G	I OZ
55 G	2 OZ
100 G	3½ OZ
110 G	4 OZ
125 G	4½ OZ
150 G	5½ OZ
200 G	7 OZ
225 G	8 OZ
250 G	9 OZ
500 G	I LB 2 OZ
I KG	2 LB 4 OZ

Note: 1 stick of butter equals 125 G (4½ oz)

LIQUID MEASURES

Metric	Imperial	Australian	US
5 ML	¼ FL OZ	I teaspoon	I teaspoon
15 ML	½ FL OZ		I tablespoon
20 ML	¾ FL OZ	I tablespoon	
30 ML	I FL OZ		2 tablespoons
60 ML	2 FL OZ	¼ cup	
75 ML	2½ FL OZ		⅓ cup
80 ML	3 FL OZ	⅓ cup	
100 ML	3½ FL OZ		
110 ML	4 FL OZ		½ cup
125 ML	4½ FL OZ	½ cup	
150 ML	5 FL OZ		
170 ML	6 FL OZ	⅓ cup	¾ cup
185 ML	6½ FL OZ	¾ cup	
200 ML	7 FL OZ		
225 ML	8 FL OZ		I cup
250 ML	8½ FL OZ	I cup	
300 ML	10½ FL OZ		I⅓ cups

OVEN TEMPERATURES

°C	°F	Gas mark
110	225	¼
140	280	I
150	300	2
160	320	3
170	340	
175	350	4
180	360	
190	375	5
200	400	6
220	425	7
250	480	8

LENGTH

Metric	Imperial
6 mm	¼ inch
I cm	½ inch
2.5 cm	I inch
5 cm	2 inches
10 cm	4 inches
20 cm	8 inches
24 cm	9½ inches
25 cm	10 inches
28 cm	11 inches
30 cm	12 inches

Some terms/ingredients used

allspice: pimento; toute-épice; Jamaica pepper

artichoke: globe artichoke

baby chickens: poussins

baking paper: wax paper; parchment paper

beef mince: ground beef

beetroot: beet

bicarbonate of soda: sodium bicarbonate; baking soda

bird's eye chillies: small hot red chillies

biscuits: cookies

broad beans: fava beans

butter lettuce: butterhead or cabbage lettuce

capsicum: bell pepper

caster sugar: superfine sugar; baker's special sugar

cavolo nero: Tuscan kale

chickpeas: garbanzos

chuck steak: stewing or casserole steak

coriander: cilantro

cos lettuce: romaine lettuce

cream, pure: light whipping cream

cream, thickened: heavy whipping cream

cream, double: heavy cream

desiccated coconut: dried shredded coconut

eggplant: aubergine

eschalot: shallot

farm cheese: farmer's cheese; block cottage cheese

flat-leaf parsley: Italian parsley

golden syrup: substitute corn syrup or maple syrup

grill (verb/noun): broil/broiler

ground almonds: almond meal

iceberg lettuce: crisphead lettuce

icing sugar: confectioners' sugar

Kipfler potatoes: fingerling potatoes; waxy potatoes

lamb forequarter chops: shoulder chops

mache: lamb's lettuce; corn salad

minced: ground

mixed spice: pie spice mix

muslin: cheesecloth

peanut oil: groundnut oil

plain flour: all-purpose flour

prunes: dried plums

rocket: arugula

Roma tomatoes: plum tomatoes

scotch fillet: rib-eye steak

self-raising flour: self-rising flour

soda water: club soda

spinach: English spinach

spring onions: scallions

sugar (regular, not caster): granulated sugar

sultanas: golden raisins; white raisins

swiss roll tin: jelly roll pan

topside mince: ground round steak

veal mince: ground veal

Vegemite: yeast extract spread

THANK YOU

Popojo, Life Inspired Jewellery, Paddington, for use of bracelets for photography; Condé Nast, for permission to use the recipe for Pumpkin seed brittle, originally published on Gourmet.com. Copyright © 2007. All rights reserved; Margaret Fulton, for permission to use the recipe for Pavlova, originally published in the *Encyclopedia of Food and Cookery* by Margaret Fulton. Published 1983; Chronicle Books LLC, San Francisco, for permission to use the recipe for Orange compote, originally published in *Fresh from the Farmers' Market* by Janet Fletcher. Text © 1997 and 2008 by Janet Fletcher.

And to the following food professionals and publications for generously sharing their recipes and knowledge, we wish to thank: Marieke Brugman (former proprietor chef of Howqua Dale Gourmet Retreat and now director of Marieke's Art of Living), Lorraine Godsmark (Yellow Bistro), Damien Pignolet (Bistro Moncur; *French*), Evelyn Rose (*The New Jewish Cuisine*) and the late Rhona Walhaus (*Jewish Gourmet Cooking*).
Recipes have been adapted or reworded from the original.

www.mondaymorningcookingclub.com.au

HarperCollins*Publishers*

First published in 2011
by Hardie Grant Publishing, Australia
This edition published in 2013
by HarperCollins*Publishers* Australia Pty Limited
ABN 36 009 913 517
harpercollins.com.au

HarperCollins*Publishers*
Level 13, 201 Elizabeth Street, Sydney NSW 2000, Australia
31 View Road, Glenfield, Auckland 0627, New Zealand
A 53, Sector 57, Noida, UP, India
77–85 Fulham Palace Road, London W6 8JB, United Kingdom
2 Bloor Street East, 20th floor, Toronto, Ontario M4W 1A8, Canada
10 East 53rd Street, New York NY 10022, USA

ISBN 978 0 7322 9780 0

Photography by Alan Benson
Design by Future Classic
Styling by Sarah O'Brien
Colour reproduction by Graphic Print Group, Adelaide
Printed and bound in China by RR Donnelley

5 4 3 2 1   13 14 15 16